Michael Manley
and
Democratic Socialism

Political Leadership and Ideology
in Jamaica

Cheryl L. A. King

Resource Publications
Eugene, Oregon

Resource Publications
An imprint of Wipf and Stock Publishers
199 West 8th Ave., Suite 3
Eugene OR, 97401

http://www.wipfandstock.com

Michael Manley and Democratic Socialism
By Cheryl L. A. King
Copyright 2003 by Cheryl L. A. King

ISBN: 1-59244-234-X
ISBN: 978-1-4982-4638-5
Publication Date: May,
2003.

To my family

ACKNOWLEDGEMENTS

I would like to express my sincere thanks to my husband , Dr. Baldwin King for his love and encouragement, to our children Bryan, Cherene and Debra who never cease to be a source of joy and inspiration, and to my mother, Eloise (Walker) Phills for always being there with her love and support.

Thanks to Professor Irving Leonard Markovitz of The Graduate School and University Center, The City University of New York for his assistance during the writing of my Master's thesis on which this book is based and thanks also to Professor William Messmer of Drew University, New Jersey for his very kind comments on the book.

CONTENTS

MICHAEL MANLEY AND DEMOCRATIC SOCIALISM

INTRODUCTION

This study focuses on the leadership of Prime Minister Michael Manley of Jamaica from 1972 when he assumed the office of Prime Minister to 1980 when he was voted out of office. It is important to study the role of Michael Manley in Jamaica's development because he was one of the first leaders to take a definite stance in terms of adopting an ideology--Democratic Socialism–which he hoped to use as a vehicle for the development of the country in the seventies. He "restored an ideology–democratic socialism–not only to the philosophic content of a party's beliefs, but proclaimed it as an ideal that informs the policies and conditions the activities of his government."[1] Michael's father, Norman Washington Manley who was the political leader of Jamaica from 1955-1962, had articulated the philosophy of the People's National Party (PNP) as being socialist in orientation in September 1940. He and a group of other middle-class politicians had founded the party in 1938. Michael became leader of the party after his father retired from active politics in 1969. The other dominant political party, The Jamaica Labour Party (JLP) which comprises the other half of the two-party system in Jamaica was founded by Sir Alexander Bustamante who was the political leader of Jamaica from 1944-1955. The JLP was the "grass-roots" party and had no basic stated philosophy at the time of its inception. The leaders of the party later adopted what was called nationalism as its political philosophy.

Between 1962 when Jamaica became independent, and 1972 when Michael Manley became Prime Minister, Jamaica had experienced growth without development.[2] Michael Manley felt that it was time to forge a new international economic order which would make Jamaica and other Third World countries more self-reliant and self-sufficient economically. He reasoned that if they could be paid more for their products commensurate with the prices they paid for their imported goods, this would be a means

---

1. John Hearne, editor, The Search for Solutions. Canada. Maple House Publishing Co. 1976. p. 27
2. See Walter Rodney, How Europe Underdeveloped Africa.. London Bogle-L'Ouverture Publications. 1972 for an assessment of this theme in Africa but which also serves well in the Jamaican situation.

1

of moving away from the dependent status inherited from the period of colonialism. Even more important in his estimation, the time had come to transform the society into a just society based on equality and opportunity. Michael Manley saw the colonial era as the root cause of the social, political and economical problems of the country. He felt that the masses had suffered enough, and thought it his duty to correct the inherent social injustices and economic imbalances left by two hundred and fifty years of colonialism, as quickly as possible. His father and Bustamante had been successful in moving the country forward politically with the formation of the two-party system, the introduction of universal suffrage (1944) and the introduction of two trade unions, the National Workers Union formed by Manley and the Bustamante Industrial Trade Union formed by Bustamante in 1939. Ultimately, the urgency with which Michael proceeded to make right the social wrongs without attaching the same kind of urgency to local production and economic growth contributed to his defeat at the polls in the election of October 30, 1980. His failure to win the elections is also interpreted as a rejection of his guiding philosophy of democratic socialism by the Jamaican people. The central thesis of this study is that democratic socialism failed because it could not deliver on the promises that were enunciated, emphasizing as it did, the redistribution of wealth rather than the production of wealth. In Jamaica (as elsewhere), the success of a political leader can be assessed in terms of his influence on the material well-being of the masses, and the ideology of the leader is an important factor in this relationship. Michael Manley's democratic socialism and non-aligned policy proved to be a deterrent to an improvement in the well-being of the masses (partly because of a lack of funds to implement his social reforms).

Michael Manley's commitment to democratic socialism never wavered, but resulted in Jamaica's estrangement from the Western world and consequent unavailability of international funds. The United States of America, in particular, was unhappy with Jamaica's close relationship with Cuba and the resulting international economic restrictions had far reaching implications for the country's domestic economy. Michael's attempts at social reform, initiated shortly after he came into power in 1972, centered on free education, work programs, minimum wages, sugar cooperatives and worker participation. These policies, though noble in intent, did not prove to be productive, economically viable undertakings. Subsidization by the government meant that more money was going out of the national treasury than was coming in. The enormity of this problem was not fully realized until the end of Manley's first term of office in 1976.

Michael Manley's overwhelming victory in the elections of 1976 was seen as an endorsement of his ideological stance, but by 1979 he found it difficult to persuade the people to be patient and to strive to overcome severe hardships such as scarcity of goods, high unemployment and poverty. His attempts to achieve his ideological objectives of equality and social justice became overshadowed by the more urgent task of trying to meet the economic needs of the country. Negotiations with the International Monetary Fund (IMF) and the seeking of financial assistance from abroad were the major pre-occupations of Manley and his regime immediately after re-election in 1976. The standard of living steadily declined during the ensuing years.

On the other hand, with the rather low-key, non-ideological stance of Bustamante and the JLP, tangible improvement in the lot of the masses could be discerned. Their "industrialization by invitation" may not have been creative or unique, but the country experienced economic growth. They antagonized no one with their foreign policy, and neither the Jamaican people nor the Western world felt threatened by Communism.

The historically colonial, structurally dependent economy of Jamaica made it difficult for Michael Manley and his Democratic Socialist ideology to succeed. In all fairness, one must agree that the oil crisis of 1973 wreaked havoc with the economies of developing nations. It might have been to the benefit of the leader and the country if Michael Manley had made some monetary compromises sooner or cut back on some of his social changes earlier. His obsession with correcting all of the social problems at once led to confusion in many programs. Rather, the implementation of well-thought out plans for a few programs might have been more impressive.

I endorse the view that the answer to development in Jamaica, given its colonial history, may be neither the capitalist nor the socialist model but a judicious selection of the more positive aspects of both systems. One positive aspect of capitalism includes preserving the profit motive while ensuring that the workers are not exploited. One positive aspect of socialism would involve the more deliberate or conscious effort of the state to take care of the needs of the down-trodden of the society, especially in areas of health care, socialization of medicine and the expansion of educational opportunities. In short, like Manley, I support the mixed economy–that is private and state ownership. Unlike Manley, however, I believe that equal emphasis should be placed on both parts.

Manley explained his position in the formulation of Jamaica's brand of Socialism this way :

The People's National Party has no intention of blindly copying any foreign formula for achieving a Socialist society in Jamaica. We are constructing our own model of Socialism which must grow out of the application of basic principles to the special nature of Jamaican society.

There are at least four such basic principles. These are:
1. The Democratic Political Process.
2. The Christian principles of brotherhood and equality.
3. The ideals of equal opportunity and equal rights.
4. Determination to prevent the exploitation of our people.[3]

Michael Manley tried to eliminate capitalism and replace it with a more openly socialist model particularly during his first term of office (1972-1976). This type of approach has been postulated by developmental theorists. Andre Gunder Frank postulates capitalism as the cause of under-development in Latin America and states that development will not take place until developing countries reject capitalism and adopt socialism. [4]The rejection of capitalism is not to be taken lightly in developing countries even those that have some commodity that is in great demand such as oil. In a country like Jamaica which is small, with few natural resources (bauxite, alumina) and a history of importing more than it exports, a total rejection of capitalism could have been even more chaotic than it actually was under Michael Manley's leadership, since he did not totally reject capitalism. The harsh economic realities make it difficult to assure the rejection of capitalism in a democratic country where election to office depends on the votes of the people. In the final

---

3. John Hearne, editor, The Search for Solutions. Canada. Maple House Publishing Co. 1976 p. 27

4. Andre Gunder Frank. Capitalism and Underdevelopment in Latin America. New York & London. Monthly Review Press 1967.
Other theorists who examine capitalism and its impact on development are Samir Amin. Unequal Development. New York & London. Monthly. Monthly Review Press. 1976
Eric R. Wolf. Peasant Wars of the Twentieth Century. NY. Harper & Row 1969
Fernand Braudel. Capitalism and Material Life. 1400-1800. NY

analysis, if the people are suffering, they will look for an alternative. The voters in Jamaica have historically embraced[5] a charismatic leader (usually the leader of either major party) in hopes of achieving a better life. The reins of power have passed back and forth between the two major political parties–the Jamaica Labour Party (JLP) won in 1944, 1949, and the People's National Party (PNP) 1955,1959, then the JLP again 1962,1967 and the PNP 1972, 1976. The JLP assumed power in 1980. This cyclical pattern will continue because third parties have not survived in Jamaica and the tradition is not one of military intervention. Carl Stone has this explanation :

> Periods of apathy, despair and hopelessness tend to be interrupted by short term millenarianism in which the rhetoric of populist leaders breaks through the wall of despair, rekindles hopes and keeps high mass mobilization at a peak for a short period. The period of upsurge is inevitably followed by extensive demobilization and a return to apathy.[6]

The appeal of the political leader is not to be underestimated in Jamaican politics. Both the JLP and the PNP initially gained power because of the personal appeal of the two founding leaders of each party. Even after Sir Alexander Bustamante retired from politics, his influence was felt at the time of General Elections. Indeed, the elections of 1972 were scheduled to coincide with his birthday. The PNP invoked the memory of Norman Washington Manley at every available opportunity. Michael Manley exuded his own personal charm and attraction. The masses idolized all three politicians.

The most important criterion for the masses at the time of elections is which party has the most to offer in terms of an improvement in their standard of living. How will they benefit ? Will they get their share of the spoils ? Which leader seems to be more sensitive to their needs ? Which leader can they trust to deliver what is promised ? The party leader takes

---

5. Since the introduction of universal suffrage in 1944. See A.W. Singham. The Hero and the Crowd in a Colonial Polity. Yale.1968

6.Carl Stone. Class, Race and Political Behavior in Urban Jamaica. ISER 1973 p. 165

all of these questions into consideration and the party prepares a manifesto (often promising more than can be delivered). What the party and party leader have found after being victorious at the polls is that it is extremely difficult, sometimes impossible to remedy the ills of the society, particularly one with a colonial heritage.

The quality of the leadership in Jamaica is very important because it is a new nation and the ideology, beliefs, and attitudes of leaders are crucial in laying the foundations for future development. That Jamaica is now a stable democratic country is due in part to its early leaders.[7] For the purposes of this study we will define leader as "one who succeeds in getting others to follow him" or " that person identified and accepted as such by his followers."[8] The new leader always has a grave task ahead in fashioning the political structures and institutions of a new sovereign nation. George Washington's task in the United States was not much different from that of new leaders today. Seymour Lipset points out that George Washington was a successful leader. A war hero, he was dearly loved by his countrymen and skillfully transformed the country from colonialism to political independence by building a strong country constitutionally. He was a strong President, and his impact on the American nation will always be felt.[9] Irish and Protho carry the sentiment even further by saying: "happily, the Commander-in-Chief of the Revolutionary forces, who was also slated to be the first President of the new republic was committed to the idea of constitutional government."[10] Happily also for Jamaica, the first two decades of national existence have seen the implementation of democratic principles under strong leaders committed to a stable, parliamentary system.

The political system of Jamaica was evolutionary rather than revolutionary from the period of colonialism to independence. The

---

7. Dankwart A. Rustow. editor, Philosophers and Kings. NY Braziller , 1970
   A compilation of studies in leadership.

8. Fred E. Fiedler. A Theory of Leadership Effectiveness. McGraw-Hill, 1959.

9. Seymour Lipset. The First New Nation. NY: Basic Books Inc. 1963 p. 18

10. Marian D. Irish and James W. Protho. The Politics of American Democracy. NJ Prentice
    Hall Inc. 1959 p.115

evolutionary process was hastened by the protests of the masses and their leaders and culminated in the achievement of independence on August 6, 1962. The problems in Jamaica are not unlike those found in other countries which have experienced colonialism and which are now in control of their own future. [11]In order to put in perspective the kinds of problems which Michael Manley inherited, I have traced the major events in Jamaica's development from the colonial beginnings in 1655 to 1972 when he assumed power.

Chapter I   - The 'awakening of the masses' analyzes the colonial era to 1938 showing the system as being responsible for the dismal political, social and economic condition of the people.

Chapter II   -'Mass mobilization and organization' analyzes the way in which the colonial system inevitably led to the upheaval of the masses as soon as their level of consciousness was raised by leaders like Marcus Garvey, Alexander Bustamante and Norman Washington Manley.

Chapter III-'The Mission of Michael Manley'-This chapter focuses on the ideas of Michael Manley before he became Prime Minister of Jamaica. His experience as a trade unionist helped to shape his great concern for the masses and their plight and the direction in which he thought Jamaica should be heading.

Chapter IV-'Michael Manley as Prime Minister' of Jamaica (1972-1980) analyzes the goals, objectives and achievements/ failures of Michael Manley and his ideology of democratic socialism through which he hoped to better the lives of the masses.

Chapter V- Outlines the general observations and conclusions of the study.

---

11. See Irving L. Markovitz. African Politics and Society. NY Free Press, 1970
The African countries which were colonized share a similar heritage with Jamaica. However, in Jamaica the inhabitants had been uprooted from their homeland and lost all trace of an indigenous culture. This was also a major concern from a national perspective.

This study has relied heavily on the works of others in the field of Jamaican and Caribbean politics. Works that have been extremely helpful are George Eaton's Alexander Bustamante and Modern Jamaica., A.W. Singham's The Hero and the Crowd in a Colonial Polity., Rex Nettleford's Manley and the New Jamaica.,Terry Lacey's Politics and Violence in Jamaica., Jamaican Leaders by Wendell Bell and The Search for Solutions edited by John Hearne. Michael Manley's "Overcoming Insularity in Jamaica," written in Foreign Affairs in October 1970 while he was leader of the Opposition in the Jamaican parliament gives us a vantage point from which to view his philosophy and plans for change in Jamaica. Although a fair amount of reading is available on the early Jamaican leaders not much is available on Michael Manley and so I have had to use much of his own works, The Politics of Change and A Voice at the Workplace to analyze his views as well as the help of newspaper articles available for that period.

It is impossible to grasp the driving force behind the actions of Michael Manley as the leader of the Jamaican people unless we understand the effects of colonialism on the country and its people. Michael Manley felt strongly that knowing the history of the country was crucial to the future development of the country. In the next chapter we will explore the past and hopefully gain some insight into the historical factors which shaped the ideological outlook of the man who became the leader of the Jamaican people during the seventies.

CHAPTER I

AWAKENING OF THE MASSES

Jamaica became a British colonial territory in 1655 having previously been a Spanish territory. After a series of struggles, there was considerable constitutional change between 1655 and 1938. What becomes clear with each set of changes is that although direct control from Britain steadily diminished, the material well-being of the masses remained deplorable.

The foundation for the evolution and development of two separate societies dates back to the ousting of the Spaniards from Jamaica in 1655. At this point, the British took all of the fertile land for the production of sugar. Many of the black inhabitants called Maroons fled to the hills and cultivated their own food. This marked the beginning of two separate economies.[12] The British established the slave plantation society based on cheap labor and institutionalized the expropriation of funds from the colonies.[13] The socio-economic situation that prevailed then has left lasting impressions on Jamaica's history and development.

Since the slaves were never wage earners, the majority were poverty-stricken. The slave was totally dominated by the conditions on the plantation. All laws came directly from England. The laws were rigid and readily enforced to keep the slaves as obedient and docile laborers. When we look at the system of government under the British during the colonial era, we can see how the masses came to be powerless in every aspect of life, as the system did not allow for their political, social or economic mobility. The powerlessness was maintained by the types of government that were instituted.

TYPES OF GOVERNMENT

The type of government which existed from 1655 to 1661 was one of

---

12. See George Beckford and Michael Witter-Small Garden....Bitter Weed. Jamaica. Maroon. Publishing House, for an analysis of "the political economy of underdevelopment in Jamaica."

13. Herein lies the basis of the structurally dependent nature of the present day Jamaican economy

9

military commissioners under military law. This was changed in 1661 to the old representative system which consisted of a Governor and a Council. The Council was appointed by the King and formed the Upper House and the Assembly formed the Lower House. These were all from the white propertied planter class who wished to maintain their power and position at all costs. The Governor played the dominant role in conducting the affairs of the colony. The "representative system" was not really representative of the whole population but was called representative because it was elected.
However:

> the electorate was very small, consisting primarily of land-owning whites, and the Assembly came to represent primarily the planting and land-owning interests, although near the end of the period some professional and mercantile interests were represented as well.[14]

The class system became rooted in the economic system and this became the basis for a racial system as well. The social structure reflected the plantation structure; sugar production meant white profits and slavery meant black cheap labor. The absentee landlords in England were forming interest groups and becoming a powerful influence in Parliament. The social and economic changes in England, the pleas of the abolitionists and the occurrence of revolutions [15]in this era were having an impact on the colonial masters and on the slaves in Jamaica. From an economic standpoint the estates were operating at a loss which necessitated a review of the production of sugar and the economic advantages of maintaining slavery. There were three main reasons for the decline in the demand for sugar from the colonies:

(1) The American War of Independence 1776 had a harsh economic

---

14. Wendell Bell. Jamaican Leaders. California Univ. of California Press 1964 p.12

15. There were the Berbice revolution of 1763 in Guyana and the San Domingo revolution in the 18th century. The French Revolution of 1789 with its slogan of liberty, equality and fraternity was having its ramifications felt elsewhere. Toussaint L'overture was successful in overthrowing the French in Haiti in 1804 which became the first black nation in the New World.

impact on the era of mercantilism.

(2) Competition from the French sugar colonies especially Santo
    Domingo (Haiti after 1804).

(3) Competition from beet sugar which was now being produced
    in Europe.[16]

The decision to abolish the slave trade (1807) may have been more of
an economic decision than an ethical decision. The slave plantation
economy was fuel to the capitalist system which emerged after the
mercantilist era. The conditions were ideal-cheap labor and maximun
profits. Political power was changing hands in England from the monarchy
and the nobles to the new monied classes.[17] The structurally dependent
nature of the Jamaican economy was established and the import/export
orientation that exists today had its foundations in this era. John Stuart
Mill described the trade relationship that existed between England and a
colony (such as Jamaica) as :

"The place where England finds it convenient to carry on the
production of sugar, coffee and a few other tropical
commodities.... The trade of the West Indies is therefore hardly
to be considered as external trade, but more resembles the traffic
between town and country."[18]

The slaves did not accept their status in the society willingly, and
showed their displeasure through revolts. The Sam Sharpe Christmas
rebellion of 1831 was the last great slave revolt before the Emancipation
Act in August 1833. The British dealt with the situation by establishing a
pattern in dealing with leaders of this kind–they were hanged.

After the Emancipation of the slaves, the Jamaican Assembly made it

---

16. George E.Eaton Bustamante and Modern Jamaica. Jamaica Kingston Publishers Limited,
    1975 p.3

17. See Eric Williams Capitalism & Slavery. N.C. Univ of North Carolina Press. Williams
    shows the relationship between slavery in the West Indies and the capitalist development
    in Britain.

18. J.S. Mill. Principles of Political Economy.London, 1892, pp.454-5

11

difficult for those who were newly freed to establish themselves in any meaningful way in the society. The land remained in the hands of the former colonial masters and the former slaves were forced to continue working on the plantations for very little. Poverty-stricken, most of them were unable to buy land or to ever think in terms of acquiring enough money to do so. The attitude of the planters to the workers was one of neglect. The workers felt hopeless and desolate. The culmination of anger which existed led to the first attempt at mass mobilization on the labor front.

The workers led by George William Gordon (a member of the House of Assembly) and Paul Bogle decided to bring attention to their plight in the form of the Morant Bay Rebellion in 1865. Once again the British eliminated the leaders of the cause by hanging Bogle and Gordon. Nonetheless, political reform and extension of the franchise were a direct result of the rebellion. The freed blacks, in a state of political inertia, let it be known that they were dissatisfied and they had no intention of remaining quiet any longer. Their ploy was effective for:

> Fear of continued disorder, combined with the prophecy that eventually the freed blacks might demand their political rights and come to dominate the Assembly, led the Assembly to give up its heretofore jealously guarded prerogatives of self-government.[19]

The struggle for better conditions had begun and this was to continue with rewarding results. The British Parliament took the opportunity to introduce some new measures. Bell observes that:

> On the British Parliament's part, a colonial administration dedicated to the welfare of all socio-economic-racial groups on the island could be established and social reforms which at that time never would have been adopted by the oligarchical Jamaican Assembly could be introduced.[20]

---

19. Wendell Bell. Jamaican Leaders. California Univ. of Calif. Press.

20. Ibid.

The struggles of the masses were finally making an impact on the direction of the lives of the people and the country. What was beginning to emerge here was a fighting spirit which would later be mobilized into genuine mass movements under leaders whose lives would be spared by the British government.

The gains were few for the masses on the whole and the old "representative" system came to an end in 1864. Crown Colony government was instituted in 1866 after the Morant Bay Rebellion. Nothing changed in terms of the seat of power which remained in the hands of the Governor. There were minor changes such as free elementary education and better medical services for the poor. There were no local leaders struggling on behalf of the poor. No one articulated an ideology aimed at improving the quality of life of the masses or bringing about social change. The pattern of plantation society remained essentially the same in Jamaica.

In Europe and the United States of America, rapid industrialization was taking place. England, with her raw materials from the colonies and ready markets for her consumer goods, flourished. In Jamaica, the new peasant class cultivated its own crops on whatever land became available. The laws of the country helped to enforce the poverty-stricken, landless existence of the majority in order to maintain a steady supply of labour on the estates. According to Beckford and Witter:

> Two kinds of laws were enacted. One set restricted the sale of land to the ex-slaves, the other set were Vagrancy Laws which were used to victimize the landless. These laws, together with heavy land taxes, served to ensure a supply of labourers who had no choice but to work for cheap wages–penny a day–on the estates. Thus, some of the ex-slaves became wage labourers and the Jamaican proletariat was born.[21]

CLASS FORMATION

At this point, it is necessary to consider the class formation of the Jamaican society in order to put in perspective the role of the brown

---

21. Beckford and Witter. Small Garden...Bitter Weed. Jamaica Maroon Publishing House 1980. p. 40

middle class as the emergent leadership group in the society. The plantation society consisted of three culturally distinct layers: the black,the brown, and the white–the blacks (Africans) at the bottom of the social scale, the browns or mulattoes (mixed) in the middle and the whites (Europeans) at the top.[22] The mulatto class occupied a privileged place over the blacks and were sometimes given lighter tasks and even educated abroad. Out of this class would emerge the indigenous Jamaican leaders.

The mulattoes found themselves in a precarious position because they were used as a buffer between the other two classes. Usually they had property and became preachers, teachers and businessmen. They had vested interests in the economy along with the many merchants consisting mostly of Jews, Lebanese and Chinese. The Jews, Lebanese and Chinese were considered to be white, resulting in what Beckford and Witter refer to as the "social power" of the classes in terms of their control over capital.[23]

The political power was also rooted in economic power because the voting qualifications were based on property. Even when the constitution changed to increase the number of representatives, the property requirement was not eliminated. Nonetheless, the political control that was totally in the hands of whites, steadily diminished. From 1906 onwards, black and colored members were elected and by 1919 there were five colored and one black in a total of fourteen.[24] Although all of this must be viewed as progress on the political level, for the most part the black population continued its existence outside of the realm of political activity and decision-making. This was soon to change. By 1920 the black and colored classes began to criticize the ineptness of the Crown Colony governments and verbalized thoughts of political advancement.

---

22. M.G. Smith. The Plural Society in the British West Indies. Calif. Univ. of Calif Press 1965.
Smith sees the divisions between the three layers of the society operating in their own spheres socially and culturally without sharing each others' interests or values.

23. George Beckford and Michael Witter. Small Garden...Bitter Weed. Jamaica. Maroon Publishing House. 1980. p.47

24.George Eaton.Alexander Bustamante and Modern Jamaica. Jamaica Kingston Publishers Limited p.4.

THE ADVANCE TO SELF-GOVERNMENT

This period marks the beginning of the assertion of a new thrust in political advancement toward self-government. The local politicians became more concerned about the condition of the masses. Many who had been abroad had returned home and shared their ideas of freedom and equality with the masses.

By 1921, the elected members and many supporters who were politically aware began to organize themselves and launched the Jamaica Representative Government Association. The political scene had opened up enough to allow for suggestions from the elected representatives. On behalf of the Association, J.A.G. Smith, a black Jamaican attorney-at-law and elected member of the Legislative Council sought constitutional reform in an effort to broaden the representative base in the society. The details of the revised constitution which he presented to Major F.L. Wood, a British Member of Parliament and visiting Under-Secretary called for the following : (1) A ten-man Executive Council with five elected members, and the Governor as President would have a casting vote. (2) A twenty member Legislative Council with fourteen elected comprising the majority. (3) Three-year terms. (4) Abolition of residential qualifications and (5) A separate nominated Legislative Council of eight members which would not be able to introduce legislation. Major Wood's reply to this proposal was that "neither in Jamaica nor elsewhere is there any demand for responsible government in the strict sense of the word nor within a measurable distance of time could such a demand rightly be conceded." [25] This reply exemplified the way in which Britain viewed indigenous leadership in the colonies. In any event, what is important is that native Jamaicans were involved in writing a constitution themselves.

J.A.G. Smith had the interests of the masses at heart and was disheartened at the response to his proposal. The British were not ready to yield too much power or influence to the local blacks in Jamaica. The Colonial Office proposed that the Legislative Council should be restructured to give the elected representatives a majority of four over the ten officials nominated by the Governor. The Governor, as a representative of the British Crown, would retain a reserve power to overrule the majority vote of the council in a matter deemed by him to be

---

25. Ibid.

15

of paramount importance. The power rested in the hands of the Governor, no matter what decisions were made by the elected representatives. The Colonial Office also proposed the creation of an Executive Committee, in addition to the Privy Council, to be an advisory body to the Governor on which a number of elected members would serve.[26]

The Council demonstrated a streak of independence by rejecting the proposals outlined by the Colonial Office. They made the decision not to become enmeshed in another powerless operation. The political situation seemed hopeless. The help that the masses needed was not coming from the British and the elected representatives were powerless. George Eaton summarizes the situation:

> The elected representatives were left with the existing
> legislative structure, within which they constituted half
> of the twenty-eight members reacting to the legislative
> initiatives of the Governor and his official slate, and in
> effect were confined to negative and destructive criticisms.
> Their major constitutional prerogative was likewise obstructive.
> Under a power of delay, if nine of the fourteen elected members
> voted against a financial measure, the motion would be defeated.
> But even so, the Governor could declare the measure one of
> paramount importance and give it legislative effect.[27]

Meanwhile, the industrialized countries with their technological advances were investing in Jamaica and utilizing the raw materials and cheap labor to make handsome profits. The age of the multi-national corporations came into being. Companies like Tate and Lyle and United Fruit Company became established. In addition to sugar there was now banana production with the help of American capital. The United Fruit Company which was instrumental in the production and marketing of the bananas, provided jobs in other export-related areas such as dock workers and clerical workers to handle all of the transactions and transport duties. With modern ships and the Suez and Panama Canal routes cutting down on distance, there was also an increase in cash crops. Many who still were

---

26. Ibid., p.18

27. Ibid.

not able to eke out an existence in Jamaica decided to emigrate and try their fortunes abroad. Panama, Costa Rica and Cuba were the most lucrative places to emigrate to between 1900 and 1930. Panama needed people to work on the construction of the Panama Canal and in Costa Rica and Cuba, labor was in demand on the sugar and banana plantations.[28]

The 1930's served as a turning point in Jamaica's history. The Depression, which affected the whole world, took its toll on the people. The prices of their primary products fell, causing ever greater hardship. The people began to lose faith in the effectiveness of the government since little was being done to alleviate their misery. Inevitably, a wave of disturbances erupted. The social forces which brought about the public demonstration against poverty and desperation are elaborated on by Hurwitz and Hurwitz:

"The basic cause of the disturbances in Jamaica in the 1930's was discontent, long latent but now intensified and brought to the surface by the economic shocks of the depression. Though unemployment, under-employment, low wages, and bad conditions had been endemic in Jamaica, the people, despite their outward placidity, apparently had not become inured to them and certainly not when the bad conditions intensified."[29]

This is the point at which the issue of leadership of the masses became most crucial. The down-trodden, poverty-stricken people desperately needed someone to help them. Marcus Mosiah Garvey became that person. He became a dominant force in Jamaica, struggling on behalf of the masses.

Hurwitz and Hurwitz explain:

Garvey was the first Jamaican political leader openly to espouse the regeneration of society. He was symbolic of a new age— the age of nationalism and self-government–which was about to be born. At an end was a period of history in which Jamaica was an administered territory subject to and governed by directives from outside itself. About to start was a period in which those who governed would respond to demands from within, from the

---

28 . George Beckford and Michael Witter. Small Garden ... Bitter Weed. Jamaica. Maroon Publishing House. 1980. p53.

29. Samuel Hurwitz and Edith F. Hurwitz. Jamaica- A Historical Portrait. 1971. p. 193.

17

masses of people.[30]

The masses were truly aroused through the efforts of Garvey. He tried to instill pride in the black man and the Negro race. During his travels abroad, he had observed that negroes held inferior positions. Through his movement, the Universal Negro Improvement Association (UNIA), black Jamaicans became more vocal and self-assertive. They could use the U.N.I.A. as a forum for articulating their problems and aspirations. His ideology of black nationalism and repatriation of black people to Africa gained momentum. For the first time, someone with a definite philosophy for the advancement of black people had been willing to devote time and energy on their behalf. When Garvey became disillusioned with the system, undoubtedly because of the lack of tangible gains for his people, he emigrated to Great Britain. Garvey left behind a vacuum as far as leadership of the masses was concerned. The landless, poor and unemployed joined with the small landowners and the few employed laborers to form a formidable group under the leadership of the flamboyant, articulate William Alexander Bustamante who had recently returned from abroad and was accepted as the champion of the people.

Garvey's influence on the masses is significant because the task of mobilizing the masses to agitate for change, was made easier because of the political awakening and self-awareness that he had stressed. William Alexander Bustamante grasped the leadership of the masses in 1938 and waged a long, hard struggle in his determination to improve the material well-being of the working people. As we shall see in the next chapter, he accomplished his mission and won the hearts and adulation of his followers.

SUMMARY

Let us now summarize the changes which Jamaica underwent from 1655 when Great Britain captured Jamaica from Spain. After one hundred and fifty years of Spanish rule, the society underwent a slight change with the establishment of a Maroon population in the hills. With the importation of slaves from Africa in the late seventeenth century, the slave

---

30. Ibid. p. 192
See Amy Jacques Garvey. Garvey and Garveyism. N.Y. The Macmillan Company. 1963. for a full account of Garvey's life and philosophy.

plantation society became firmly established.

During this era, the Governor was in direct control of the affairs in Jamaica. Between 1655 and 1938 the country passed through various political stages but the material condition of the masses remained virtually unchanged.

The political changes were as follows:

(1) 1655-1661- Rule by military commissioners under military law.

(2) 1661-1865- The old representative system consisting of a Governor and a Council appointed by the King.

(3) 1866-1895- Rule by a Governor and a Legislative Council consisting of nine elected members.

(4) 1895-1938- Rule by a Governor and a Legislative Council consisting of 14 elected members. This existed beyond 1938 until 1944 when a new constitution came into effect.

Although the slave trade was abolished in 1807, the Emancipation of Slavery did not take place until 1838.

The year 1865 was a landmark in Jamaican history with the Morant Bay Rebellion. After the Emancipation of the slaves in 1838, the abominable conditions which prevailed left the workers with no choice but to show their displeasure in the form of revolt. The leaders of this rebellion, Paul Bogle and William Gordon (a member of the House of Representatives and the planter class) were hanged by the authorities.

The 1930's saw the appearance of Marcus Mosiah Garvey as the leader of the poor, black, dispossessed workers. Garvey with his philosophy of black pride was instrumental in the political awakening of the black masses. When Garvey left for Great Britain in 1935, a new politically aware black populace waited for a messiah. William Alexander Bustamante, recently returned from abroad, emerged as that messiah and struggled relentlessly on behalf of the masses for an improvement in their life. Strikes and demonstrations were used as vehicles to bring about change in the Jamaican society. The masses were willing to pay the price and allowed themselves to be led by a man in whom they had implicit faith. They trusted him and clung to him as their only hope for survival.

CHAPTER 2

MASS MOBILIZATION AND 0RGANIZATION

Jamaica, in 1939, was a country that had made a few political
advances, but not much was accomplished in terms of social and economic
advances. The colonial system had set the stage for future change under
leaders who were sensitized in the colonial era. William Alexander
Bustamante first came to the public's attention through his letter writing in
the daily newspaper, The Daily Gleaner. He was an avid writer and wrote
incessantly about the social issues of the day. From the time he wrote his
first letter in April 1935, he was perceived as a man who had the interests
of the masses at heart.[31] He and Norman Washington Manley were able to
achieve political gains on behalf of the people. It is necessary to follow the
constitutional development of the country in order to see how the two
dominant leaders of the 1930's–William Alexander Bustamante and
Norman Washington Manley – were able to play such an important role in
Jamaican politics during this period.

One hundred years after Emancipation, the Apprenticeship scheme that
was to allow for the easy transition of the newly freed people into the
mainstream of the society was not achieving its aim for the majority.
Rustow points out that "the need for leadership–is proportional to the
distress of the followers.[32] " The Jamaican society was in chaos for this
was the time of world-wide Depression, (1930's) and the need for
leadership was great. On May 23, 1938 the workers were in disarray
following a series of strikes and revolts. Bustamante, while addressing the
dockers who were demanding higher wages stated that they were
experiencing a mental revolution and not a military revolution. On May
24th , he attempted to address a crowd at Spanish Town Road, but police
intervened and broke up the meeting. One hour later, he proceeded to the
Fire Brigade Headquarters where the firemen were also having some
problems. He proceeded to the Mayor's office to plead their case. As he
passed the police headquarters, Bustamante was stopped and placed under

---

31. George E.Eaton. Bustamante and Modern Jamaica. Kingston Publishers Ltd. 1975 p.24
    Bustamante's letter was political in tone. He mentioned the right of the unemployed to
    demonstrate to bring attention to their condition and warned the Government not to use
    force against the people.

32. Dankwart A. Rustow ed., Philosophers & Kings. NY Braziller 1970 p.21

arrest. This simple action turned Bustamante into the people's hero. The Longshoremen stopped working and refused to go back to work until Bustamante was released. Bustamante had reached the stage of indispensability.[33]

Norman Washington Manley, a prominent lawyer and Bustamante's cousin, came to his rescue and thereafter was a moving force on the political scene. Bustamante was released shortly thereafter and he and Manley travelled throughout the island negotiating on behalf of strikers. As Bell points out "both (men) have a clear claim on the title 'father of the nation,' but each one must always share it to some extent with the other."[34] The charisma of these two men shaped the course of political development for the country.

According to Weber, "charismatic authority repudiates the past, and is in this sense a specifically revolutionary force."[35] Bustamante and Manley complemented each other and changed the direction of Jamaican politics. They established many of the basic political institutions which exist in Jamaica today. In September 1938, Manley, in cooperation with other middle class leaders, launched the Peoples' National Party (PNP). Two years later, Manley declared that it was a socialist party. The chief objectives of Manley were a call for universal suffrage and the attainment of independence and nationhood for Jamaica.[36]

Manley's political action was followed by trade union organization. Bustamante announced plans for organizing five unions under the name "Bustamante Industrial Trade Union." (BITU). It was felt that if the workers were organized into a movement, they would attain more control over their own affairs and if they had more control over their own affairs

---

33. George E. Eaton. Bustamante & Modern Jamaica. Kingston Pub., Ltd. 1975 pp.42-46.

34. Wendell Bell. Jamaican Leaders. California Univ. of Calif. Press 1964 p.17
Both of these men, along with Paul Bogle, William Gordon and Marcus Mosiah Garvey were named the first five national heroes of Jamaica.
See Sylvia Wynter. Jamaica's National Heroes. Jamaica. Jamaica National Trust Commission 1972.

35. Max Weber. Theory of Social and Economic Organization. NY 1947 p. 358

36. George E. Eaton. Bustamante & Modern Jamaica. Kingston Pub. Ltd. 1975 p.67

then this would enable them to live a better life.[37]

Although Bustamante was very popular, he accomplished little in the ensuing years. He seemed to have no definite plans for development of the country, the party or the union. There was very little effective organization or real achievement. Great Britain, once again, thrust him in the forefront. Bustamante made a speech in which he attacked the colonial authority. Britain was at war at the time and had no desire to be criticized by anyone, let alone a colonial subject. He was forthwith imprisoned. He was now perceived as a martyr by his followers and his place in the hearts of the people was secured.

During the seventeen months that Bustamante was imprisoned, Manley took on the task of organizing the union. Soon, membership rose from eight thousand to twenty thousand. Manley also negotiated the first all-island sugar agreement in March 1941. All subsequent sugar negotiations emanated from this original document. The relationship between Bustamante and Manley was dissolved in 1942. After Bustamante was released from prison in February 1942, he went on a campaign denouncing everybody. He was afraid that Manley was trying to usurp his power. A year later he launched the Jamaica Labour Party (JLP). Thus, the dominant two-party system which exists today was brought about as a result of a personality conflict between Bustamante and Manley. [38]The seeds for a vibrant two-party, Westminster model, democratic system were now sown.

Manley later went on to form the National Workers Union. In what developed to be a unique situation, the BITU became affiliated with the JLP and the NWU with the PNP. That relationship has also endured to this day. Eaton sums up the distinction between the two political camps as follows:

> The Bustamante Industrial Trade Union and later the Jamaica Labour Party became the institutionalized expression of working-class discontent and protest, while the Peoples' National Party embodied Manley's belief in the efficacy of organized politics and

---

37. Ibid. pp.70-72

38. Ibid. p.88

22

the ability of the Jamaican people to determine their own destiny.[39]
Bustamante and Manley had worked well together for the benefit of
Jamaica and Jamaicans. Bustamante had the uncanny ability to arouse the
masses and Manley had the intellect, creativity, ability and skill to
formulate and implement policy. The indigenous leaders took the initiative
in outlining what they considered to be a model for governing the country.
Hurwitz and Hurwitz state:

"In October 1942, a proposal for a new constitution was put forward in
a joint memorandum by three groups, including all fourteen of the elected
members of the Legislative Council, three representatives from the
People's National Party and three representatives from the Federation of
Citizen's Association.... They called for a bicameral legislature-an elected
lower house or House of Assembly and an upper house to consist of
nominated and ex-officio members. The reserve powers of the governor
were to be limited. The governor would not have any power of certification by paramount power and his veto power ...could be exercised only
under limited specified conditions. Of an Executive Committee of ten,
seven were to be elected by the lower house and three were to be officials
nominated by the governor. The Committee was to be the principal
instrument of policy, with power to initiate all laws, financial and
otherwise. It was expected that the Executive Committee would develop
into a Cabinet along British lines and that subsequently its name would
bechanged to Council of Ministers. To further this end, the members of the
Executive Committee who came from the lower house were to be placed
in charge of specific administrative departments and their authority
gradually extended. One resolution called for the setting up of a Jamaican
civil service." [40]

The PNP now took a leading role in politically activating the general
public. Fearful of persistent and possibly dangerous agitation, prodded
also by demands in the United States that Britain introduce democratic
reforms in its Caribbean empire, the British Government yielded; and in a
rejection of the Moyne Commission's recommendations, the Colonial
Office agreed to most of the Jamaican demands. The Moyne Report was
the report of a Royal Commission that was appointed to examine the

---

39.Ibid. p.234

40. Samuel J. Hurwitz and Edith F. Hurwitz. Jamaica. A Historical Portrait 1971. p.202

social, economic and related matters in Jamaica and other Caribbean territories. The Commission did not recommend self-government, and industrial development was not held in high regard. Nonetheless, on February 23rd, 1943, Colonel Stanley, Secretary of State for the Colonies, stated that Britain was now ready to introduce "far reaching constitutional advances" in Jamaica. A new chapter in Jamaican history was initiated with the inauguration of a new constitution in 1944.[41]

The efforts of the two political agitators were paying off. At the same time, the British Government was not yet prepared to give up its complete control over the colony. In the new Constitution it therefore reserved the power, when it deemed it necessary, to exercise that control. The Governor was retained with respect to the power of veto, reservation and certification, to be exercised when it became expedient in the interests of "public order, public faith, or good government," and the definition of the term was, of course, left to the Governor. He could thus "certify bills that he deemed necessary without the consent of the legislature, and he had, also, the negative power of veto and disallowance. Despite the promise of far-reaching constitutional advances, the British Government did not give up all control.[42]

In the new constitution, the House of Representatives was to be comprised of thirty-two members elected by Universal Suffrage with no literacy or property requirement. That had been one of Manley's objectives. The maximum duration of the House of Representatives was five years. A plurality was necessary for election. The Upper House- the Legislative Council- was comprised of official and nominated members who had deliberate and delaying powers. The Executive Council, later called ministers, was to be "the principal instrument of policy" under the Constitution. There was also a Privy Council or advisors to the Governor, whose main function was to advise the Governor on matters of discipline and his judicial prerogative.[43]

Under this new system, it was impossible for the Jamaicans to handle their own affairs totally although they did have a considerable degree of

---

41. Ibid. p.204

42. Ibid. p.203

43. Ibid. p.204

self-government. Under unusual circumstances, complete and unrestricted power was to be exercised by the Governor (as the representative of the British Government). The Executive Council, which was the principal, and in effect, the sole instrument of policy, had no individual party functions of responsibility nor any direct executive authority. The central Secretariat was headed by the Colonial Secretary. The new constitution went into effect on November 20, 1944.[44]

The first general election under this new constitution was held on December 14, 1944. Earlier , Bustamante had founded the Jamaica Labour Party (JLP) as the political arm of the BITU and this established the beginning of the two-party system in Jamaica. The charismatic appeal of Bustamante prevailed over Manley and the JLP won the first general election and formed the first government that was elected under adult suffrage. According to Bell:

> The JLP received 41.4 percent of the 389,109 votes cast (663,069 persons were eligible) for twenty-two of the thirty-two seats available in the House of Representatives. The PNP secured 23.5 percent of the votes for five seats, but Manley lost in his own constituency. The five remaining seats were won by independent candidates.[45]

Democratic politics in Jamaica had made tremendous progress. The new legislature held its first session on December 9, 1945. The JLP won again in the 1949 election. The PNP won in 1955 and 1959, after an attempted change in Manley's image. Bell elaborated on the change in strategy in promoting the image of Manley, the leader of the PNP:

> In 1949 when 65.2 percent of the 732,217 eligible voters went to the polls, the PNP got 43.5 percent of the total votes to the JLP's 42.7 percent, but owing to the distribution of constituencies, the JLP still controlled the House with seventeen seats. The PNP created its own labor union linkage with the establishment of the National Workers Union in 1952, and deliberate efforts were made to enhance Manley's popular appeal largely by

---

44. Wendell Bell. Jamaican Leaders. Calif. Univ. of Calif.Press 1964 p.17

45. Ibid. p.18

the manipulation of his public image. Dissatisfaction with the JLP government grew, the PNP opposition was active in the House, and throughout the island the PNP engaged in an organizational campaign. In 1955, the PNP swept into office with 50.5 percent of a popular vote of 495,680 which resulted in eighteen PNP seats. The JLP with thirty-nine percent of the popular vote won fourteen seats.[46]

Norman Manley became Chief Minister in 1955. In 1952, the popularly elected House of Representatives had unanimously supported a resolution calling for self-government and indeed constitutional changes took place in 1953, 1956, 1957 and 1959, all leading to more self-government.

In 1958, Jamaica became part of the ill-fated, short-lived Federation of the West Indies. This Federation consisted of nine other Caribbean territories - Antigua, Barbados, Dominica, Grenada, Montserrat, St. Kitts-Nevis-Anguilla, St. Lucia, St. Vincent and Trinidad. Federation was thrust on the people of Jamaica, as well as the other islands of the Caribbean, by the British. It was felt that the Federation was a ploy used by the British to get rid of the islands since they had out-lived their major function as a producer of primary goods and the importer of manufactured goods. It was no longer profitable to the mother country to maintain these colonies; if anything, they had become liabilities. The British insisted that this path was the only feasible one to independence. The matter became a hotly debated issue between the two parties. - Manley for Federation, Bustamante against it.

In the general elections of 1959, the PNP won 54.8 percent of the total votes (to the JLP's 44.3 percent) for twenty-nine of the newly enlarged forty-five seat House of Representatives. Manley decided to let the people vote on the issue of Federation, and called a referendum, in September 1961. The people voted against Federation, and Jamaica withdrew its membership. The consensus of opinion was that Jamaica should seek independence on its own. This outcome shattered Manley, as he strongly believed that he would have won on this issue. [47] As Bell explains:

---

46. Ibid. p.19

47. Ibid. p.19

"The largely antifederation rural vote outweighed the urban profederationists, and of 473, 580 total votes 45.9 percent were for federation while 54.1 percent were against. Thus, the voters had decided that Jamaica would "go it alone". Personally saddened, Manley had little choice but to begin negotiations for Jamaica's separate independence, which he began at once with a bipartisan committee, and to call another general election so that the country would have the party of its choice to lead it into full nationhood."[48]

A third party now emerged - the People's Political Party (PPP) - led by Millard Johnson, a Jamaican. "His political appeal included a clear racist theme."[49] He placed a great deal of emphasis on racial equality. If we look at degrees of facial complexion among the three men, Bustamante was near-white, Manley light-brown and Johnson dark-brown. The emphasis on race received great importance during the campaign, but as the election results showed, it had little effect. In the general election held in April 1963, the PPP got "less than one percent of the more than half-a-million total votes, the PNP and the JLP together getting 98.6 percent...But the PNP government fell, capturing nineteen seats to the JLP's twenty-six. [50] Jamaica's three centuries of colonial status came to an end on August 6, 1962 when the country became an independent nation. William Alexander Bustamante became the first Prime Minister of the independent nation. The years of agitation, struggle and imprisonment had paid off, although by this time he was almost eighty years old.

INDEPENDENCE CONSTITUTION

The constitution of independent Jamaica bore traces of the colonial experience. A parliamentary system modeled after the British parliamentary structure, was established. Parliament had an Upper Chamber called the Senate, which was comprised of twenty-one appointed

---

48. Ibid. p.20

49. Ibid.p.20

50.Ibid. p.20

members. Thirteen members were nominated on the advice of the Prime Minister, and eight on the advice of the Leader of the Opposition. The Senate which was formerly the Legislative Council, had limited powers. Parliament also had a Lower Chamber called the House of Representatives which was comprised of 58 elected members corresponding to the number of constituencies. Elections for the House were held at the discretion of the Governor-General on the advice of the Prime Minister. The intervals between elections must be no more than five years. The Governor-General, whose role was largely ceremonial and was the Head of State was appointed by the Queen of England on the advice of the Prime Minister. Executive power was vested in the Cabinet led by the Prime Minister.

The Judiciary was also modeled after the British system. The Court of Appeal was comprised of seven members who were appointed by the Governor-General on the advice of the Prime Minister, in consutlation with the Leader of the Opposition.[51] There was an elected Parish Council on each parish. Kingston & St. Andrew had joined together (forming KSAC). This Council exercised limited governmental responsibilities.

Self-government brought to an end British political and military control. From 1937-1938, when "there was wide-spread malnutrition, inadequate housing, few educational opportunities for the average Jamaican, widespread poverty and unemployment and spreading resentment, discontent and agitation among the Jamaican masses as well as among some middle-class Jamaican intellectuals," [52]to 1962 when independence was achieved, the struggle was continuous. With Bustamante and Manley at the forefront, the expectations of all were high that a better life lay ahead. The people looked forward to a new political system, but as Terry Lacey states in Violence and Politics in Jamaica 1960-70:

The personalism of Jamaican politics combined with the weakness of party and union organisations was bound to create a matrix of patron-client relationships as the dominant feature of the political

---

51. The Jamaica (Constitution) Order in Council, 1962
   Jamaica's constitution reflects the influence of British colonial rule on the institutions of the country. The indigenous leaders, having been socialized and educated in the British tradition used this expertise and experience in promoting constitutional changes over the years.

52. Wendell Bell. Jamaican Leaders. Calif. Calif. Univ. Press 1964. p.23

system. Although the PNP organisation strengthened during the decade, the decision to select Michael Manley to replace his father as its leader reflected the way in which the lives of a mere two men, Norman Manley and Alexander Bustamante, had profoundly affected Jamaican politics.[53]

SUMMARY

The socio-economic underdevelopment of Jamaica had tremendous influence on the political development of the country. Many believed that Bustamante and Manley, the emerging leaders in the 1930's would ameliorate the economic and social conditions of the masses. Both leaders hoped to improve the material well-being of the masses and struggled on their behalf from 1938 until they became legitimate leaders elected under universal suffrage (which was instituted in 1944). Alexander Bustamante was elected the first Chief Minister in 1944 and Norman Washington Manley became Chief Minister in 1955. Both men were instrumental in bringing about political change (such as universal suffrage and self-government). This was done through constitutional changes in 1944, 1949, 1953, 1956, 1957 and 1959. Jamaica became part of the Federation of the West Indies in 1958. This collapsed after the people of Jamaica voted against this type of association in a referendum held in September 1961. Jamaica then moved on to become an independent nation on August 6, 1962.

The dominant political structures and institutions in independent Jamaica evolved around the two prominent leaders. The formation of the two main political parties–the People's National Party (Manley) and the Jamaica Labour Party (Bustamante), the Bustamante Industrial Trade Union (Bustamante) and the National Workers Union (Manley) are a direct result of the personality conflicts that arose between these two leaders. Both men were concerned with the quality of life of the masses and in their own way sought to alleviate the burden and suffering of the working man. The pre-occupation of the British Government with the effects of the 1930's depression at home and then the Second World War gave the indigenous Jamaican leaders an opportunity to move forward without devastating interference from abroad. The struggle was far from over, but Bustamante and Manley accomplished their political mission as

---

53. Terry Lacey. Violence and Politics in Jamaica.. Frank Cass & Co., NJ p.46

far as the political awareness of the masses was concerned. Social and economic rehabilitation were left to leaders like Michael Manley who came later.

CHAPTER 3

THE MISSION OF MICHAEL MANLEY

When Michael Manley, the son of Norman Washington Manley, came to power as Prime Minister of Jamaica in 1972, Jamaica had experienced almost a decade of independence. During the period since independence the Jamaica Labour Party had promoted what they called the idea of "Nationalism." They also supported foreign investment in a rapidly expanding economy.[54] By 1972, in their quest to establish an identity, they were promoting a policy of "Jamaicanization."

The task of governing during the sixties centered around the building and maintaining of political institutions in the country. Norman Manley, at a banquet honoring him on his seventy-fifth birthday on July 4, 1968, recounted what had been accomplished in the past and what needed to be done in the future. He said:

My generation had a distinct mission to perform. It was to create a national spirit with which we could identify ourselves as a people for the purpose of achieving independence on the political plane. I am convinced, deeply convinced that the role of this generation is to proceed to the social and economic reform of Jamaica.[55]

Clearly, he perceived the mission of his successors to be one of instituting fundamental changes on the social and economic fronts. That was precisely what Michael Manley set out to do.

Michael Manley may have taken on too much too soon, but he proceeded on his quest for social and economic justice with a passion. He was a new kind of politician. Hearne explains :

Unlike Bustamante, the elder Manley etc. who were sucked into a political vacuum relatively late in life, and who had to learn their professionalism while creating a nation, the younger

---

54. The JLP embarked on a policy of "industrialization by invitation" as was patterned after the Puerto Rican Model.

55. See John Hearne editor, The Search for Solutions. Can Maple House Publishing Co. 1976 p. 5

breed–Michael Manley, Edward Seaga, Hugh Shearer etc. have come consciously prepared to a profession which can no longer be filled merely by the accidents of charismatic presence, or of burning conscience, but which must recruit early, those who have a talent for it.[56]

Indeed, a new breed of young politicians had become active in both political parties. The PNP under the leadership of Michael Manley (1969) and the JLP under the leadership of Hugh Shearer (1967) attracted a great deal of support from all segments of the society. Although Hugh Shearer, the former Prime Minister, was admired by the Jamaican people, he never aroused the fervor that was evident with the election of Michael Manley in 1972. Michael Manley had the appeal of Bustamante to the masses and the skill and intellect of his father.

Michael Manley made his debut as a political candidate in 1967 and won his seat as the representative for Central Kingston. Before that, he was an active member of the National Workers Union (NWU). In order to get a clearer picture of the situation in Jamaica when Manley came into office as Prime Minister, it is necessary to review the course of events during the 1960's. "The main course of political events reflected the fierce struggle of the JLP government to consolidate its power in a hostile environment.[57] The predominant themes centered around the "have vs. have-not" speech of Edward Seaga in April 1961 and the widening gap between the two groups. [58]Accusations of job victimization against JLP and BITU supporters were levelled at the PNP.[59] Political violence was growing into a very serious problem.[60] Each party had its various strongholds. (This trend and its associated violence has continued to this

---

56. Ibid p.15

57. Terry Lacey. Violence & Politics in Jamaica 1960-70 USA Frank Cass & Co. 1977 p.46

58. Ibid.

59. Ibid.

60.Ibid.

day). Lacey continues:

> The most bitter power struggles in the period, 1966-7 were
> between politicians who perceived a power vacuum in their
> respective party leaderships and realized, that the restraining
> hand of the 'dynamic duo' had weakened with age. The
> weaponry of political warfare thus changed from rhetoric to
> the Molotov Cocktail and the gun.........[61]

By 1967, political violence had become a part of the Jamaican political
system and was of major concern to Acting Prime Minister Donald
Sangster[62] and Prime Minister Hugh Shearer (who held office until 1972).
Both parties made joint efforts to try and restrict the violence but without
success.

For five years after independence Jamaica experienced relative social
stability and economic growth. Four companies went into alumina
production and many small businesses appeared. Industrialization seemed
to be moving at a rapid pace.

The elections of 1967, for the first time since the introduction of
universal suffrage in 1944, was free of the Bustamante/Manley personal
confrontation. The struggle now was between Donald Sangster and
Norman Manley but Bustamante's influence was still to be felt. The JLP
set the elections to coincide with his birthday and they won 33 of the 53
seats. In his victory statement, Sangster said: "I will follow the broad
guideline laid down by Sir Alexander, subject to the changing patterns of
life in our society.[63] Sangster died of a brain haemorrhage shortly
afterwards, before he could be sworn in as Prime Minister. Hugh Lawson
Shearer who had already succeeded Sir Alexander Bustamante as leader of
the BITU and representative in the Clarendon seat became the Prime
Minister of Jamaica.

What started out as a period of advancement in industry, social reform

---

61. Terry Lacey. Violence & Politics in Jamaica 1960-70 USA Frank Cass 1977 p.46

62. Donald Sangster fell ill in March 1967 and died in April 1967. He had succeeded
    Sir William Alexander Bustamante who had retired on account of ill health.

63. The Jamaican Weekly Gleaner. (N.A.) Monday, August 11, 1980 p.30

and international trade ended in internal disagreement among members of the government.

The problem of violence was of immediate concern to the new Prime Minister. As Lacey observes:

> This last part of the decade was characterised by four related main themes which pointed to the guts of the Jamaican political system indicating that violence was an integral part of it. These themes were : rising discontent over unemployment and job victimization; increasingly bitter industrial disputes exacerbated by inter-union rivalries, the breakdown or disruption of public services, and the continued growth of industrial, political and criminal violence.[64]

The country was plagued by strikes and industrial disputes [65]and there was the added complication of "black power" emerging as an area of political conflict. When Dr. Walter Rodney, a radical black Guyanese university lecturer was banned from Jamaica, violence erupted. Lacey states:

> The political impact of the Rodney affair was that it opened many eyes as to the extent of the divisions within Jamaican society and the possibility that a radical black power movement might mobilize 'the sufferers' against the main political parties– In the long term the most important political consequence of the Rodney affair was that Norman Manley, at the end of his political career, embraced the concept of black power, so gaining for his party and his successor a base from which to redefine black power in non-violent terms and to build a bridge between an increasingly isolated political elite and a growing grass-roots political culture.[66]

---

64. Terry Lacey. Violence & Politics in Jamaica 1960-70. USA Frank Cass & Co. 1977 pp.50-51

65. Ibid pp.51-52

66. Ibid p.52

When Norman Manley retired in 1969, the PNP came under the leadership of Michael Manley. He was considered by many as charismatic, forceful and as a man with new ideas for the development of the country. The PNP "played upon every weakness of the JLP and introduced in Michael Manley a rebirth of the messianic politics of Bustamante and Norman Manley. The tired, divided JLP was no match for the new PNP in 1972."[67]

The problems of crime and violence, unemployment and the high cost of living, were of paramount importance at the end of the sixties. Lacey summarizes:

The fundamental political problem dominating this period was the inability of the economic system to provide jobs. The crises and tensions which flowed from this basic economic inadequacy account largely for the type of political issues generated by these tensions related to civil liberties or constitutional issues because the style of political leadership in these circumstances tended to be personalistic, defensive and under Shearer, heavy-handed.... Simultaneously there was serious controversy over the operation of the electoral registration system and accusations and gerrymandering.[68]

By the end of the 1960's, the JLP was unpopular with the masses who looked to the PNP for leadership. A cyclical pattern began to emerge between the two parties. After two terms of JLP government the people were ready for a change. Of great importance was the fact that :

The PNP reached for the political leadership of the nation by

---

67. The Jamaican Weekly Gleaner (N.A.) Monday, August 11, 1980 p.14

68. Terry Lacey. Violence & Politics in Jamaica.1960-70, USA Frank Cass & Co. 1977 p.53
Lacey mentions some of the civil liberties issues such as seizure of passports in the public interest, the banning of literature, the use of prohibition or exclusion orders against black power leaders, the use of section twenty-six of the Immigration Restriction (Commonwealth Citizens) Act against non-Jamaicans in Jamaica (by which non-Jamaicans could be excluded from landing in Jamaica even if previously resident there).

establishing itself as the vehicle for the legitimate aspirations of the black people of Jamaica, by seizing from the JLP the initiative as the party of redistribution, which Michael Manley achieved in June 1968, with his own 'have and have-not' speech-and by championing civil liberties and constitutional rights.[69]

Michael Manley, as leader of the Opposition in the Jamaican Parliament in 1970 had very definite views on what he perceived to be the problems of Jamaica. In an article in Foreign Affairs entitled "Overcoming Insularity in Jamaica", Michael Manley recognized that the crux of the problem had to do with economics. He wrote:

In the long run it may yet transpire that the differences between stages of economic development as between various nations and regions of the world are a more important determinant of history than differences in ideology or systems of government.[70]

The problems of Jamaica, as he saw them, all resulted from the effects of colonialism. It was, therefore, of the utmost importance to restructure the economy. He wrote:

....Our economy has remained firmly cast in the colonial mold. The bauxite and alumina industry is entirely North American owned. More than half the tourist and sugar industries are under foreign ownership. Foreign trade continues to grow faster than internally consumed production and remains oriented toward traditional lines of exchange with North America and Great Britain. And those who manage the economy continue to look outward for ideas and expertise. In spite of dramatic expansions in the bauxite and tourist industries, a balance-of-payments situation in surplus and the rapid development of a sophisticated network of financial situations and a basically sound civil service, Jamaica remains a prey

---

69. Ibid. p.54

70. Foreign Affairs. October 1970 p.100

to many of the evils which beset it in colonial times.[71]

He also was concerned about the high rate of unemployment and the low production rate in agriculture. The matter of foreign capital was of great concern. In terms of the tensions that existed in the society among the young people, he wrote : "In short, they feel that we are sacrificing economic independence for the explicit purpose of solving our internal problems, but that in the event, since the problems are growing worse, the sacrifice is in vain."[72]

What were Michael Manley's plans for restructuring the economy ? We will look at his suggestions of solutions under the following headings: (1) Land reform (2) Industrial development (3) Foreign capital (4) Joint Ownership (5) Unemployment and (6) Regionalism.

On Land Reform Manley writes:
A largely agricultural country, Jamaica is exporting J $62 million of sugar, bananas, citrus and coffee, while it imports J $60 million of food, and this in a context where some 20 percent of its arable land is either totally idle or seriously under-used....[73]

On Industrial Development Manley writes:
----Much of the industrial development of the last 20 years has been of the last stage assembly "screw-driver" type, while virtually no attention has been paid to agro-industrial development, which is the most obvious area for establishing inter-industry linkages. The total result has been that agriculture, while supporting more than half of the population, contributed 13 percent to the gross national product in 1960 just before the attainment of independence, but only nine percent in 1969.[74]

On Foreign Capital he writes:

---

71. Foreign Affairs. October 1970. p. 100

72. Foreign Affairs. October 1970. p.104

73. Foreign Affairs. October 1970. p.105

74. Foreign Affairs. October 1970 . P.105

Broadly speaking, Jamaica has fallen into the same trap as many other developing countries by thinking that the indiscriminate granting of tax incentives to foreign capital regardless of the contribution which the particular capital can make to development, or of the posture of that capital in the society–will necessarily contribute to progress. [What is needed is] ...a complete reexaminaton of the sort of foreign capital which should be invited to participate, and the relationship between foreign capital and the national interest as regards ownership and control.[75]

On Joint Ownership he writes:
Even in recent times, when experiments in forms of joint ownership ventures between foreign and local capital have become the vogue in response to nationalist pressures, there is still no evidence of realistic national planning as to the sort of ventures that are needed, and, in particular, industries which seek to exploit local raw materials and by-products.[76]

On Unemployment he writes:
If unemployment is to be significantly reduced and the dangerous gap between the agricultural population and the industrial elite is to be narrowed, radically different policies have to be pursued. These will have new thinking about the use to which internal resources are to be put.[77]

On Regionalism he writes :
As a consequence of the federal experience, Jamaica is undergoing a period of ambivalence toward the rest of the Caribbean. In less fanciful terms, the party in power, the Jamaica Labour Party (JLP) is hostile to regionalism partly in response to the parochial instincts which lay behind its anti-federal fight and partly because it is a prisoner of its success in that fight. The opposition People's National Party (PNP) tends to be afraid of regionalism because its own loss of power was attributed to its support of federation in the 1961 referendum–what is needed, I suggest, is a tough-

---

75. Ibid.

76. Ibid.

77. Ibid.

minded recognition that national survival, like business survival, is a matter of margins and that regionalism can provide the framework in which internal markets are increased, external bargaining power enhanced and international recognition maximized."[78]

Another of the over-riding concerns for Michael Manley was the increase in crime which led to the formation of a commission on crime.[79] With all these problems in mind the PNP campaign for the 1972 general elections became a campaign of promises with the slogan, "Better Must Come." There were promises for better roads, more housing, more water, more clothing, less unemployment, no victimisation, land reform, a just society based on the 'politics of participation,' greater security (because the gunmen were a group to be dealt with severely). The message from the party was:

The PNP will destroy the guns. We will find them wherever they are. We will take them from those who should not have them. And we will destroy them. We will put an end to the constant roar of the criminal gun. We'll silence them once and for all. We'll ensure that the police enforce the law, And let the gunman pay for his crimes. This we solemnly pledge.[80]

The grievances were many and the PNP used these effectively to mobilize voter support. The party leader, a natural orator, capitalized on the issues of 'joblessness, victimization, corruption, low levels of living and general economic discontent which grew cumulatively during the JLP's ten year term of office.[81] " According to Stone:

Two important factors facilitated the PNP's capacity to mobolize

---

78. Foreign Affairs. October 1970 p.106

79. Terry Lacey.Violence and Politics in Jamaica. 1960-70 USA Frank Cass & Co. 1977 P.53

80. The Jamaican Weekly Gleaner (N.A.) Monday, August 11, 1980 p.30

81. Carl Stone. Class, Race and Political Behavior in Urban Jamaica. Jamaica ISER 1973 p.169

the disaffected. The first was the large inputs of financial, material, and symbolic resources, which the Party received from crucial interest groups which were alienated by certain JLP policies... The second factor facilitating the PNP recovery was the force, strength and appeal of the image of its new leader Michael Manley. Manley was projected in the PNP's campaign as a "brown" populist leader with the paternalistic stature of the biblical "Joshua" who promised radical but vague changes in the conditions of life faced by the masses and was sympathetic to the cultural and racial aspirations and expressions of the black masses through his symbolic association with Rastafarianism.[82]

The JLP policies had alienated the crucial interest groups, especially the business sector, a group which can hardly be antagonized because of its importance to the economy of the country. Stone states that:

The traditional JLP alliance with the business sector, which has been largely an alliance with the merchant class, soured as a consequence of the JLP tax policies, control and regulation of the manufacturing sector. The Jamaicanization policy of nationalization of, and antagonism towards the foreign owned utility companies controlling telephone and electricity services...The JLP lost the support of the local churches on the issue of the National Lottery And church leaders gave openly partisan support to the PNP.[83]

The leader-personality trait in Jamaican politics dominated the campaign. Lacey states that "the style of Manley was simply far superior to that of Shearer, and the 'politics of participation' was bound to be victorious despite JLP propaganda efforts such as the 'Get the Facts' Meeting."[84]

Therefore, the people rallied behind the PNP and the party ended up

---

82. Ibid

83. Ibid.

84. Terry Lacey. Violence & Politics in Jamaica 1960-70 USA. Frank Cass & Co.1977 p.54

with an overwhelming victory on February 29, 1972. PNP won 37 seats and JLP 16. Michael Manley, leader of the PNP was sworn in as Prime Minister on March 2, 1972. As Prime Minister, he now had the opportunity to fashion Jamaica according to his own philosophy. He said:

> I totally distrust these cliche words like socialism, capitalism and this, that and the other. I don't know any socialist country in the world that is not in fact employing a kind of capitalism as part of its total fabric. I don't know any capitalist country that isn't employing socialism. I think the labels have become totally irrelevant to the contemporary situation.[85]

Now the people waited for their deliverance.[86]

SUMMARY

When Michael Manley won the elections of 1972, the overwhelming victory of his party (37 seats to the JLP's 16 seats) was interpreted as a mandate by the people to deliver on his "better must come" campaign slogan. Michael Manley as leader of the opposition in the House of Representatives and son of Norman Washington Manley was seen as a new type of politician combining the earthy, grassroots touch of Bustamante with the skill and intellect of his father.

Michael Manley saw the root cause of all problems in Jamaica in colonialism. Since the political mission of political independence had been accomplished, he saw his mission as that of achieving social justice and economic independence. With definite ideas on land reform, industrial development, foreign capital, unemployment, regionalism and crime in mind, he set out to change the Jamaican society in the decade of the seventies, secure in his role as leader of the party and the country and with the full support of the masses.

---

85. The Jamaican Weekly Gleaner (N.A.) Monday, August 11, 1980 p.30

86. Michael Manley had been hailed as "Joshua" during the campaign. There was talk of the Rod of Correction. The deliverance theme was—"Thus it was in this land saved by the Almighty hand. Something written in History new/ The Great Deliverance of '72."

CHAPTER 4

MICHAEL MANLEY AS PRIME MINISTER

Michael Manley first became involved in politics as an activist in the Trade Union Movement. In 1955, he was elected First Vice President of the National Workers Union, a position which he held until 1972 when he became Prime Minister of Jamaica. He was elected President of the Caribbean bauxite and Mineworkers Union in 1962, and was appointed to the Senate that same year. In 1967, he became the PNP representative in Parliament for the people of Central Kingston. He was elected President of the Party and appointed Leader of the Opposition in 1969 after his father, Norman Washington Manley, retired from politics. For seventeen years Michael Manley had been actively involved in fighting the cause of the worker. [87]His success in the 1972 elections was due largely to the art of personal persuasion, he was regarded by the masses as their savior. Stone explains:

Manley stimulated an intense level of mass excitement, involvement and millenarian expectations for change, which temporarily trans-formed the low-key style of politics which characterized the post-independence period. In contrast, the JLP leader Hugh Shearer projected a weak, lower-middle class conservative, anti-black, unsophisticated and ineffectual image as a party leader.[88]

With the overwhelming support of the people in 1972, Michael Manley proceeded to administer his government. He was surrounded by a group of young, active, dedicated people and everyone's expectations were high, that, indeed, in the words of the PNP campaign slogan, "Better must come."

Michael Manley immediately embarked on the politics of transformation. His primary objective was to improve the way of life of the most socially, politically and economically oppressed members of the society. He placed priority on education for, in his words, "education is

---

87. For an in-depth account of Manley's activities as a trade unionist see Michael Manley. A Voice at the Workplace. London. Andre' Deutsch Ltd. 1975

88. Carl Stone. Class, Race and Political Behaviour in Urban Jamaica. ISER. p.171

the key to what must be an act of self-transformation.[89] " In his view, political freedom and economic freedom could only be brought about if one had the necessary qualifications and skills to support the requirements of a new society. His task, as he saw it, was to achieve social justice based upon equality. To him, it seemed that the "process of transformation from stratified to a classless society must begin with the educational process."[90] He also believed that the educational system should be relevant to the society and be a reflection of the society's needs and goals.

Two years after becoming Prime Minister Michael Manley in his Budget Debate Speech made at Gordon House on 29th May, 1974, outlined his plans for improving the lives of the masses, as follows:

1. Indigent allowances to be increased from $4 to $5 a fortnight.
2. Basic pension under National Insurance Scheme to be increased from $3 to $4 a week.
3. Pension of Government pensioners to be increased by amounts up to 50 percent.
4. Statutory Board workers to receive increases of up to 20% to April, 1973
5. Reclassification for Local Government employees.
6. Salary increases for nurses.
7. Substantial adjustments in mayor's and councillor's allowances.
8. Agricultural Marketing Corporation outlets moving into low areas.
9. Sidewalk vendors will find a home in proper street markets.
10. A new Mental Health Law to be passed.
11. A Family Court to be established.
12. Compulsory recognition of unions, no victimization of workers; collective bargaining would be required with compulsory reinstatement of wrongfully dismissed workers.
13. Workers through their Trade Unions would own , operate and enjoy resort cottages on the best beaches.
14. $2 million to be spent to build five complexes for small

---

89. Michael Manley. The Politics of Change. A Jamaican Tesament. London. Andre'Deutsch, 1974.

90. Ibid., p.159

43

businessmen.

15. 31,000 young people projected to get two years training after primary school.
16. Free school uniforms to be provided for the 450,000 primary school children
17. Free education for handicapped children.
18. 10,000 farmers to receive good land under Project Land-Lease
19. Young people to be trained as farmers on prime land at Montpelier
20. Sugar workers to own prime sugar lands co-operatively at Frome/Monymusk and Bernard Lodge.
21. A subsidy of 33 1/3% on the prices of all fertilizer to assist the farmers in their undertakings.
22. $37 million to be paid by Government on Government work projects to help the unemployed.
23. The introduction of a Minimum Wage Law and standard working hours for workers effective December 1, 1974.

He summed up his speech by saying that "in 1974 we are trying with God's help, to make our contribution to the movement forward for our people and the quality of their lives."[91]

Manley continued with his (socialist) social reforms even though unsurmountable administrative and economic obstacles surfaced in the process of implementation of these projects.

1974 was the year of the articulation of Manley's "democratic socialist" ideology. In November 1974, Michael Manley explained the rationale for the acceptance of his philosophy as the guiding principle in the Jamaican situation:

> The People's National Party is committed to the belief that people perform best when they do so of their own free will. For that reason, we believe in democracy, in democratic institutions, in Parliament and the rule of law. Democracy aims to give each person an equal chance to play a part in the free election of Governments and the making of policy in the nation. Socialism

---

91. Budget Debate Speech by Michael Manley 29/5/74 API Jamaica pp.66-68.

is designed to give each person an equal opportunity in life to pursue happiness, to achieve fulfillment and to contribute to the nation. Therefore, democracy and socialism must go together to build a nation where people have equal rights and opportunities. The PNP is dedicated to equality. Therefore, the PNP is dedicated to Democratic Socialism.[92]

In 1974, no one could have foreseen what was going to happen to the Jamaican economy as the government embarked on subsidizing most of its social programs. As a result, the country faced economic problems. This undoubtedly stemmed from short-sightedness in the area of economic planning, which was consistent with Manley's belief that economic plans must focus on people rather than on things. Manley had said:

It is not surprising that we have paid far more attention to the statistics of growth than to the figures of unemployment; nor is it, I suppose surprising that the fact that unemployment grew faster than the economy seems to have occasioned little alarm. If, however, we accept that economic growth is not an objective in itself but a result to be desired to the extent that it creates the conditions within which to pursue full employment and a rising standard of living for everyone, then we have introduced an important new criterion against which to measure our planning options. Let us therefore bear constantly in mind our two prime objectives of full employment and the distribution of wealth designed to reduce the gap between rich and poor and achieve a kind of economic development that is general rather than exclusive in its impact.[93]

By 1976, at the end of Manley's first term Jamaica was in the midst of a serious financial crisis, the severity of which the nation was unaware. In September 1976, Manley made his "We are not for Sale, We

---

92. John Hearne ed. The Search for Solutions. Canada. Maple House Publishing Co. 1976 pp. 158-159

93. John Hearne ed. The Search for Solutions. Canada. Maple House Publishing Co. 1976 p.130

know where we are going" speech. The results of the December 15, 1976 elections made him even more confident of his ideological stance. There were now 60 constituencies . The PNP won 47 seats and the JLP won 13 seats. This overwhelming victory was interpreted by many as the stamp of approval for the continuation of development along the democratic socialist, non-aligned path. Accordingly, Manley proceeded to have drawn up an Emergency Production Plan under the aegis of the National Planning Agency. With the euphoria of the victory of elections over, the dismal, destitute economic situation of the country was brought to the fore. Thus Manley came to the end of a fairly successful first term in terms of positive social change for the masses, but the resultant devastating economic problems became the preoccupation of his second term and eventually led to the defeat and failure of the Manley regime.

In January 1977, Manley confirmed his party's commitment to self-reliance through democratic socialism. When Manley announced in Parliament on April 22nd, 1977 that his government would have negotiations with the International Monetary Fund (IMF) for monetary assistance, the decision was met with disagreement from several quarters even within the PNP itself. Concern was uppermost in the minds of the people and other nations in the Caribbean, especially Trinidad and Tobago, which feared the control and power that the IMF would have over the country. So much for self-reliance and the input of the Nation Planning Agency's plans based on the opinions of the people. From 1977-1980, negotiations with the IMF became the pre-occupation of the Manley government, and the philosophy of democratic socialism appeared to have lost its fervor. Economic chaos resulted in social and political chaos and the defeat of the PNP in the General Election of 1980.

Of utmost importance to the chaotic economic situation was the international outlook and in particular the American response. Unlike the earlier postulations of self-reliance, non-alignment, sovereignty, and the right to determine one's own destiny, the economic crunch forced Manley to seek better relations with the United States of America. Various attempts were made to be cordial to the United States especially since there was now a new administration under Jimmy Carter.   Andrew Young, the United States Ambassador to the United Nations was known to be sympathetic to the Caribbean countries and to Jamaica, in particular, now in dire economic straits. The foreign exchange situation in Jamaica was now crucial because the business sector, frightened by all of the socialist dogma slowed down activities and the banking system started to suffer. The central bank was almost depleted of funds as many people found ways of sending their money out of the country, legally and illegally. This put a further financial drain on the economy and later when thousands of skilled nationals emigrated, this resulted in a serious brain drain (which a young developing country can ill afford at any time.)

The country was now in an economic bind which affected every other aspect of life in the nation. Social change was feeling the effects and the material well-being of all was on a downward trend. An agreement was signed with the IMF in July 1977 which called for a 40% devaluation of the Jamaican dollar providing a two-tier exchange rate using the old rate for certain basic goods. Five months later the government was negotiating with the IMF again and in December 1977 the former agreement was suspended because of a technicality. The next five months of negotiation saw the country on the road to bankruptcy, unable to pay its foreign debts. When a new agreement was reached in May 1978 the terms were catastrophic but the government had no alternative. Over the next three-year period the following steps were to be taken:

1. 15% devaluation immediately and monthly devaluations of 1.5%
2. Wage restraint with ceiling of 15%
3. Private sector guaranteed profits with a floor of 20%
4. State Trade Corporation (which had been instituted for government to have some control over imports) had to cut back its operations.
5. Government expenditures and participation in the economy were to be restricted and to operate under tight budget management.
6. Projected $180 million in new taxes.[94]

These restrictions would cause undue hardships to everyone, in general, and to the masses, in particular. Indeed, this had been of great concern to the government. Mr. P.J. Patterson, the Foreign Minister of Jamaica, met with Mr. Michael Blumenthal, the United States Secretary of the Treasury in March 1977 and explained the effects that devaluation as advocated by the IMF would have on the economy.

It was explained that devaluation would not have been

---

94. George Beckford & Michael Witter. Small Garden...Bitter Weed. J.A.Maroon Publishing House 1980. p.94

appropriate in the context of an unemployment level of
some 23% as this would increase prices, especially for food,
increase unemployment and would inevitably have placed an
intolerable burden on the most disadvantaged groups in this
society.[95]

From this point on, the economy continued on its downward trend. The
overtures for American help continued. There were two obvious public
displays of American concern for Jamaica in 1977. Mrs. Rosalyn Carter,
the wife of the President, visited Jamaica and Andrew Young visited in
August. Finally, in a more tangible vein, the United States Agency for
International Development presented a loan package of US $63,400,000 in
November 1977. In December 1977, Prime Minister Michael Manley met
with President Jimmy Carter. The whole of 1977 was spent trying to
function and coming to terms with the severe economic problems that
existed. 1978 followed the same pattern as 1977.

In January 1978, consistent with the regulations of the IMF, the
Jamaican dollar was once again devalued and the government grimly faced
the realization that the country's ability to produce and export enough to
meet its foreign debts was far below expectations. As was the concern of
many, the IMF now dominated the scene in Jamaica. Another international
organisation, the World Bank , acted as a sort of economic insurance
policy by chairing a lending consortium. [96]The harsh economic conditions
which existed did not leave much leeway for action when it came to the
implementation of social programs. There was disaffection with the IMF.
The people continued their debates on the pros and cons of the kind of
assistance they were receiving. The media covered the subject extensively.
Much to the advantage of the JLP, the people started losing faith in the
PNP government. (The letters IMF were jovially referred to as "It's
Manley's Fault.")

There was widespread discontent as everyone started to suffer from
shortages of basic items. Manley was losing support from every class in

---

95. See Jamaica. Hansard-Parliamentary Proceedings of the House of Representatives Session
    1977-78, Vol.2 No.3 (13 January 1977-12 April 1977) p.156. Michael Manley in his
    Speech The Economic Crisis that was broadcast on Jan.5, 1977 had also expressed the
    same sentiments).

96. Daily Gleaner. May 19, 1978.

addition to the business sector. The skilled professionals were leaving the country and not being replaced, a serious situation for a developing country. Manley continued with his ideological stance still hopeful that the United States would come to his assistance with more substantial financing.

In July of 1978, a United States Economic Mission paid a visit to Jamaica to look into what they called "the investment climate" in Jamaica.[97] This seemed like another attempt to show some tangible form of concern of the United States for the economic crisis which now existed in Jamaica, but there was no solution to the huge problems. 1978 was an economic fiasco.

The international economic crisis created domestic disillusionment and disaffection among the Jamaican people and by January 1979, a road block demonstration was staged with the help of the Opposition. The issue was the price increase of gasoline. At the same time, the country was unable to pass the IMF "tests" and the middle class was becoming increasingly uneasy because of the lowering of living standards.[98]

On the local political scene, the Workers Liberation League, (WLL) a Marxist group led by Dr. Trevor Munroe, a University Lecturer, became a political party in December 1978, known as the Workers Party of Jamaica. The PNP now found itself in the middle of the JLP (right) and the WPJ (left). The PNP now found itself in a compromising position with the communist section of the party aligned with the WPJ, and the leader of the party still trying to maintain a progressive, somewhat neutralist stance in an attempt to keep the support of the middle and lower classes. Ideologically, Manley's democratic socialism was uppermost in his mind as he realized that it was becoming increasingly difficult to survive without the help of the capitalists. The merchant class was crumbling and there was a critical shortage of the necessary basic food stuff. The suffering of the people was articulated in their music and vividly demonstrated with a dramatic rise in crime and violence. The social base

---

97. "US Economic Mission Comes," Daily Gleaner, July 26, 1978.

98. "Middle Classes Caught in Cross-Fire, says PM," Daily Gleaner, February 3, 1978.
    IMF-Jamaica negotiations were chronicled in a paper by Dr. Vaughan Lewis
    entitled, "The Small State Alone: Jamaican Foreign Policy, 1977-1980" delivered to the
    Annual Conference of the Caribbean Studies Association held in Jamaica, May 25-29,
    1982.

of the party was gradually diminishing, and the Opposition was ready and willing to mobilize the masses who were also ready and willing to be mobilized.

In June 1979, the new agreement with the IMF involved collaboration between the Government and the Opposition primarily because of the trade union affiliation to the two major political parties. When Michael Manley tried to impose wage guidelines as directed by the IMF, this was vigorously opposed by the Opposition. Thereafter, the country was plagued by industrial disputes.

As December 1979 approached, it became clear that the country would fail the IMF test, and it did. Thereafter, there was considerable debate as to whether the country should withdraw from the IMF route altogether. In March 1980, the Cabinet voted to break off negotiations with the IMF. By this time, the Opposition JLP had organized itself well enough to have regained the confidence and votes of the people. Manley was forced to call elections as a result of the gloomy economic outlook and the disaffection and disillusionment among the masses (who had reiterated as a result of all the shortages of food-stuff and high unemployment and lack of social change that, "Bitter Has Come.") On October 30, 1980, the JLP which had won only thirteen seats in the previous election, now became victorious by a land-slide victory. The JLP's task as explained in its manifesto was to reverse the domestic and foreign policies which had left the country in chaos, and to regain the former close ties with the United States.

The Cuban connection was a major factor in the defeat of the PNP. The Cuban problem only became crucial during the second half of Michael Manley's term as Prime Minister. Indeed, as early as September 1973 Michael Manley had displayed an affinity with Fidel Castro, the Cuban leader when they had travelled to Algeria as supporters of the Non-Aligned Movement.

Through his policy of Non-alignment, Manley had hoped to achieve closer contacts with the Socialist bloc of countries. This new area of trade and collaboration made people suspicious of the terms of the friendship, especially in view of the fact that Cuba was so close to Jamaica, geographically. Many believed that the close contact which Manley hoped to achieve extended beyond trading affairs. There was further speculation when Fidel Castro visited Jamaica on October 16, 1977. The Opposition did not participate in any of the activities in which Castro was involved. They claimed that the visit was not handled in a manner that took into account the feelings of the people of Jamaica who "feel a deep abhorrence and a profound distrust of communism in any form."[99]

In November, Mr. Hugh Shearer, who was the previous Prime Minister of Jamaica, stated that the government policy of recruiting men to be sent to Cuba with the stated objective of receiving technical training in housing construction should be stopped immediately, because "the young Jamaicans recruited are really being indoctrinated in Communism and Communist organisational techniques."[100]

Not only was Cuba very much in the forefront in its relations with Jamaica, but contact between the Jamaican government and Russia had progressed to the extent that a Russian technical team arrived in Jamaica in November. An agreement was signed between the two countries in which the Soviets would offer their help in constructing a cement plant with a capacity of approximately 500,000 tons per year. The Foreign Minister, P.J. Patterson, who was the guiding force behind these discussions, termed the arrangement as "another milestone in the further development of economic and technical cooperation between Jamaica and the USSR with regard for "the principles of respect for sovereignty, national independence, non-interference in each other's domestic affairs, equality and mutual benefit."[101]

Prime Minister Michael Manley proceeded to Yugoslavia in November 1977 and thence to Hungary in December 1977. It now seemed like a frantic effort to gain monetary assistance from any country regardless of its political philosophy and at the same time asserting the sovereignty of independent Jamaica to pursue its course of non-alignment. After a visit in February 1978 from the Cuban Foreign Minister, the Communist threat remained and the Opposition used it to its full advantage.

Edward Seaga succeeded Hugh Shearer as leader of the JLP and seized the opportunity to recharge his forces, to rebuild the party and seek support nationally and internationally as well. In April of 1977, while on a trip to Europe, he pointed out that his efforts would be devoted to the waging of a "peaceful resistance" campaign against the Government in

---

99. Fidel Comes Today "JLP to Boycott Castro's Visit, "Daily Gleaner, Oct.16,' 77.

100. Shearer: Socialism Will Not Motivate People to Produce, Daily Gleaner, 11/2/77.

101. "Jamaica-Russia Sign Pact" Daily Gleaner 11/29/77 also "Wide Range to be Explored in Soviet-Jamaica Talks," Ibid.

the form of (1) Boycotting the opening of the next Parliamentary Session. (2) Making it known to Amnesty International and the International Commission of Jurists the violations of human rights by the Government.[102]

The Opposition also highlighted the Government's association with Cuba, implying the Cuban model of development was preferable to the Puerto Rican model where the present government was concerned. The Cuban influence and communist overtures permeated and scared the nation at large and the private sector in particular. They decided to organize themselves by forming the Private Sector Organisation of Jamaica (PSOJ).

By early 1979, all of the Cuban and communist talk had begun to take its toll. When the Government announced on March 20th, 1979 that Prime Minister Manley was to make an official visit to Russia from April 9th to 14th, [103]the Private Sector Organisation of Jamaica (PSOJ) organized themselves and took a strong stand, expressing their fears of communism and communist links to the International Communist Movement. The JLP also grasped the opportunity to announce that the government intended possibly to embrace Marxist Communism while operating in a one-party state. These allegations were steadfastly denied by the Central Executive of the PNP.[104]

What did the Prime Minister achieve through his visit to Moscow ? (1) Agreements relating to the sale of alumina to Russia (50,000 tons) between 1980 and 1983 and 250,000 tons per annun subsequently (2) Assistance towards the construction of a cement plant (3) The granting of a long-term loan by the USSR to Jamaica that would finance imports from

---

102. Complaints focused on the State of Emergency which lasted for almost one year- June 19, 1976- June 6, 1977. Allegations of malpractices in the General Election of December 1976, and the charge that supporters of the JLP were being victimized.

103. "PM to Visit Moscow April 4-15," Daily Gleaner. 3/21/79

104. PSOJ Tells PM About Fear of links with World Reds,Daily Gleaner.3/24/79
PNP Faces A Cross-Roads Decision, Daily Gleaner, 3/26/79. "Private Sector Denounced by PNP," and "Communism No!" Daily Gleaner 3/28/79.

the Soviet Union[105]. Manley seemed pleased but the rest of the nation and the Opposition, in particular, were not. To add to all of the disgruntlement at home, Trinidad and Tobago expressed concern about this new agreement and this resulted in some distance being placed between Jamaica and Trinidad/Tobago. The other CARICOM members were not overly concerned with the economic plight of Jamaica. To make matters even worse, Foreign Minister Patterson visited Cuba shortly afterward to discuss among other things "certain aspects of collaboration with Cuba arising from the recently concluded trade agreement with the Soviet Union."[106]

When a new Cuban Ambassador, Ulisses Estrada Lescalles, arrived in Jamaica, the Opposition took exception to his appointment, claiming that he had been a member of the Cuban secret service and they feared that he might intervene in the politics of the country. The Prime Minister came to his defense trying to allay fear of Cuban encroaching communism in Jamaica. Afterwards, the Prime Minister attended the Non-Aligned Movement Conference in Havanna in September 1979. The economic situation at home was grim, and the chief source of assistance, the United States, was in the middle of ratifying the Panama Canal Treaty which was turning out to be quite costly. The added aggravation of Soviet Troop maneuvers in Cuba led to the expansion of American naval activities in the Caribbean. (Also of American concern were the events in Nicaragua where there was opposition to the Somoza regime, and the Soviet invasion of Afghanistan at the end of 1979). The American situation at this point in time was one of continued antagonism to Cuba, and disapproval of the action of the Soviet Union. That Jamaica was seemingly friendly to both Cuba and the Soviet Union did not help in improving relations with the United States. Therefore, when Eric Bell, Minister of Finance, went to the United States in September of 1979 seeking aid, it was not surprising that no funds were forthcoming. Jamaica's debts at this point were overwhelming but Manley persisted in maintaining his non-aligned stance. His address at the Non-Aligned Conference in Cuba September 3-9, 1979 seemed to be the forum for an attack on the United States. The Carter

---

105. "Prime Minister's Account of Deals with Russia and Hungary," Daily Gleaner. April 20,1979.

106. "PJ Off to Cuba For Talks," The Daily Gleaner, 4/19/79

Administration acted promptly to show its disapproval according to Ben Meyer:

> Secretary of State Cyrus Vance expressed privately the U.S. Government's displeasure at Manley's comments and actions when he invited Jamaica's Foreign Minister, Percival Patterson, to a closed-door conversation in Washington a few weeks ago. The circumstances suggest a blunt warning that such things were counter-productive, from every aspect, in a country which has shown a desire to help Jamaica.[107]

Indeed, in the final analysis, what brought down the Manley regime was the withdrawal of financial support by the United States. The Opposition now became very happy with the situation. With every financial avenue closed, with strained relations with the IMF, criticisms from the PSOJ, the Opposition, the media and the masses, it was too late for the Government and the party to recover and Manley must have realized then that the world is divided into power blocs and non-alignment might work but not forever. Even his relentless advocacy of a New International Economic Order, plausible though it may seem, did not meet with much success. As he himself summed it up the morning after his defeat in the General Election of October 1980, "What we did was challenge the power of the Western economic structure. This was one country that tried to challenge hegemony and was not successful."[108]

SUMMARY

Michael Manley won the General Election of 1972 with a broad base of people's support; the PNP won 37 seats to the JLP's 16 seats. His seventeen years of trade unionism had exposed him to the problems of the workers and he proceeded to make social amends on their behalf with remarkable zeal.

The first two years in office saw the projection of social reforms along the lines of minimum wage, increase in pensions, free education and land cooperatives. In 1974, Manley announced that the road to development

---

107. Ben Meyer, "Pretty Little Jamaica becomes a Big Worry," Daily Gleaner, 11/11/79.

108. "Victory in Jamaica Exceeds Forecasts," New York Times. 11/1/80.

would be through the democratic socialist path. Through democratic socialism he wished to bring about equality and social justice and to preserve the sovereignty of Jamaica based on non-alignment. Manley won the General Election of 1976 overwhelmingly and this was interpreted as a sanction of the ideological stance of Manley and the PNP.

From 1977-1980, the country was plagued with economic problems. Manley's close attachment to Cuba and Fidel Castro antagonized the United States of America and resulted in the drying up of international funds. Scarcity of basic food stuff at home led to disenchantment with the government. The rise in crime made matters worse. Nonetheless, Manley continued on the non-aligned socialist path, and made visits to Hungary and the Soviet Union in search of better trading pacts but unfortunately this was not enough.

Negotiations with the International Monetary Fund (IMF) plagued Manley's second term from 1977-80. The requirements of the IMF, such as devaluation of the Jamaican dollar and the placing of a ceiling on wage increases, created a stir among the local people. Finally, talks with the IMF were suspended. The Opposition had used the dismal economic situation coupled with a communist scare to rebuild its forces. The situation in Jamaica seemed chaotic with balance of payments problems, increase in crime, shortage of basic food items and high unemployment, the 'better must come" slogan on which the party had campaigned had not materialized, and the people were ready for a change. On October 30, 1980, Michael Manley and the PNP were voted out of office overwhelmingly. Manley and Democratic Socialism had lost favor with the people because of a failure to produce tangible evidence of a better life. The main thrust of Manley's government seemed to have been social reform, with a redistribution of the existing wealth of the country rather than a generation of new wealth.

CHAPTER 5

CRITIQUE OF THE MANLEY YEARS

Michael Manley failed to accomplish his stated goals of economic independence and social reform to the degree that he had anticipated. In view of the abysmal economic situation that existed during his term of office as Prime Minister (1972-1980), his ideology of democratic socialism failed . The reasons for this failure were as follows: (1) A tremendous imbalance existed between the social and economic reforms which he sought to implement. His emphasis on social reform pointed to a redistribution of the existing wealth (of an already poor country). Too little economic reform meant little or no improvement in the capacity of the economy to generate new wealth. This , in turn, meant that he had to rely extensively on external financial aid to meet the needs of the country whose economy had historically been dependent on external inflows of capital. (2)The international forces had a tremendous impact on national objectives. (3) Manley's anti-imperialist, pro-Cuba foreign policy not only antagonized the Western powers, particularly the United States of America, but domestically created fear of a communist style government. This instability led to the exodus of money and skilled workers which stymied whatever little economic reform he proposed. Manley was caught in a vicious cycle; the money he needed to implement his social policies was being sought from the very sources which he so blatantly and eloquently denounced. To expect the international, United States-influenced organizations (such as the International Monetary Fund) to be favorable to his position was to be truly idealistic (if not simplistic).

The basic capitalist-oriented nature of the Jamaican economy made it difficult for the people to overcome the psychological obstacles and embrace democratic socialism. The masses had struggled long and hard to achieve a better way of life, the middle class had become accustomed to a certain standard of living and the upper class was resistant to any kind of change.

Since the introduction of universal suffrage in 1944, the policy of industrialization by invitation (or the Puerto Rican Model) was the strategy for development followed by both the JLP and PNP regimes. However, Michael Manley viewed the Puerto Rican model as self-defeating. In his view, the dependence on foreign capital meant that from an economic stand-point, the country was still in the same position as in the colonial years, except that the masters were now of a different nationality. In this sense, one can see the basis for his repudiation of

56

imperialism and his insistence on sovereignty and non-alignment for Jamaica.[109] From a purely philosophical viewpoint, many of his ideas were good, but in a more practical vein his reforms, instituted in the name of "democratic socialism", led to economic disaster.

Michael Manley thought that Jamaica, as an independent country (already a decade old when he came into office), was ready to dictate new terms of operation to the international corporations doing business in Jamaica. He had felt that the limited resources of Jamaica were being exploited by multi-national corporations. Indeed, when we look at the bauxite-alumina industry, the sugar industry, the banana industry and the tourist industry (all vital to Jamaica's economy), we note that they were all dominated by foreign interests. When Manley increased the bauxite levy and tried to get a bigger share of the other industries through nationalization, production fell in each case. The move was counter-productive. The period from 1962 to 1972 under JLP leadership, showed that the Gross Domestic Product (GDP) "had virtually doubled in real terms." However, in the period from 1972 to 1981, the GDP had declined a cumulative total of 25%.[110] Unemployment also worsened under Manley's leadership moving from 24% in 1972 to 26.8% in 1980.[111]

The downward trend of the economy was due to (1) the oil crisis. When the Arab countries decided to increase the price of oil in 1973, Jamaica was directly affected because it "is 97% dependent on oil for energy."[112] (2) A steady decline in export production. Sugar declined from a peak of 500,000 tons of sugar in 1965 to 70,000 tons in the seventies.[113]

---

109. See Michael Manley. The Politics of Change-A Jamaican Testament. Lond. Andre' Deutsch 1974 p.21
   Manley refers to the psychology of dependence as "the most insidious, elusive and intractable of the problems which we inherit."

110. Michael Manley. Jamaica. Struggle in the Periphery. Great Britain, Oxford Univ. Press. 1982, p.173

111. Ibid, p.173

112. Ibid, p.150

113. Ibid, p.150

(3) The production of bauxite and alumina fell and the prices also fell. (4) Tourism was on the decline partly due to the tremendous increase in crime. (5) Exportation of funds by Jamaicans, many of whom were skilled. A managerial and financial vacuum was created when they emigrated. The country never recovered from this brain drain. (6) Importation of goods (food, equipment, raw materials and other necessities) far exceeded the cost of the exports.

In addition, most of the programs instituted by Michael Manley and funded by the national treasury were non-productive or a source of conflict; for example (1) Attempts at Land Reform were not economically viable and emphasis on participation in decision-making did not have the expected results of motivating the people to produce more for themselves. (2) The institution of a Mimimun Wage Law which should have been beneficial to workers at the lowest scale of the social strata, forced the middle classes to find alternative solutions to their child-care problems. As a result, the lower strata suffered more (financially) than they had before the introduction of this law. (3) The National Housing Trust introduced in 1977 whereby workers and employees together contributed to help with low and middle income housing led to conflict in the area of distribution. (4) Manley's expansive educational policy, which made education free (including university education), turned out to be extremely expensive and even his plan for university graduates to do national service fell through. The National Literacy campaign succeeded in graduating more than 200,000 with literate and numerate skills,[114] but the monetary returns to the government were minimal. (5) The institution of the Gun Court to deal with severe crimes was a source of consternation to the people who felt that democratic and human rights were being violated. (6) The State Trading Corporation that was established (so that government could be directly involved in the importation of products thereby assuring the best prices and establishing new trade links) did not have the support of the private business sector which later formed their own organization-the Private Sector Organisation of Jamaica (PSOJ). (7) The introduction of the new property tax (which was based on the improvement to land or property) was designed as a mechanism for the redistribution of wealth. However, farmers were exempt from any such tax. Property owners were appalled. (8) The Labour Relations and Industrial Disputes Act designed

---

114. Ibid. p.77

to give the workers a fair hearing in cases of dismissal, caused concern particularly among employers. The age old Masters and Servants Law which had existed since colonial times was being replaced by more progressive worker's right-based laws. Women were to be given equal pay for equal work . (9) Attempts were made to relieve unemployment by introducing service work such as beautifying the streets, by cleaning and planting flowers, running day care centers and basic schools. Manley admitted that there "was much in the programme that was wasteful and which angered not only the oligarchy and the middle classes and even parts of the trade union membership."[115] (10) The government's decision to take over the public utilities did not help to make things run smoothly, and there was constant trouble with power shortages particularly (11) The government became involved in the tourist industry at precisely the time when tourism was on the way down. World-wide inflation and the prevailing crime situation in Jamaica did not help the tourist trade.

(12) When the Manley government decided to acquire the only cement factory in the country, the building and construction which had been taking place at a tremendous rate in Jamaica went into a slump. There was opposition from the private sector in this takeover and Manley himself said that the whole situation "became a battleground."[116] (13) What generated much debate was the Cuban involvement in the Jamaican society. When sixteen Cuban doctors arrived to help with health care and other Cubans arrived to help build the Jose Marti school, the communist scare seemed to increase by their physical presence. The Opposition Party-the JLP, ever-vigilant, used the precarious economic situation and the threat of communism to full advantage. They were able to convince people that their freedom was being taken away slowly. Manley's adamant denial of a pending communist take-over made no difference. In fact, the people lost faith and credibility in the Manley government.

A general assessment of the Manley era (1972-1980), prior to the 1980 elections, showed a gloomy state of affairs with no improvement in the near future. During 1980, there was a 54% decline in the Gross Domestic Product (in constant price terms). The Gross Domestic Product per capita (constant prices) declined 6.5%. During the first six months of 1980, there

115. Ibid, p.92

116. Ibid, p.94

59

was an increase of 16.9 percent of the general price level as indicated by movements in the consumer price index. The rate of unemployment in April 1980 was 27.9 percent. In terms of industrial relations, the first month of 1980 showed two hundred and seventy-one reported disputes, of which there were seventy-one stoppages. The manufacturing sector declined 12.4 percent in 1980.[117] In addition to the decline in bauxite and alumina production, sugar production also declined partly due to smut and rust disease. Banana exports declined due to the effects of hurricane Allen which severely damaged the banana plants. Because the economic outlook was grim, unemployment high and shortages of basic food stuff prevailed, the masses withdrew their once popular support for Manley and democratic socialism.

Manley tried to use his leadership and ideology to dislodge the vested interests of the oligarchy which he saw as having emanated from the period of colonialism. His effort to redistribute the wealth more equitably did not materialize. His eloquent enunciation of his ideology was more rhetorical and idealistic. Indeed, his were new ideas through which he sought to reorder the Jamaican society. Whereas the Jamaica Labour Party administration placed great emphasis on economic productivity with its industrialization by invitation strategy, Manley's government emphasized social justice and equality. The basic ideology was not adequately articulated, much less implemented; there were different interpretations of democratic socialism from different sectors of the Peoples' National Party. The predominant mode of economic organization centered around agrarian reform. However, the Jamaican people have traditionally stayed away from the land in favor of white collar jobs. It may be that the colonial heritage instilled in the people the feeling that upward mobility meant moving away from agriculture and the land. Manley may have underestimated this deeply held notion. The work ethic in the field of agriculture was hard to arouse.

Manley felt that colonialism had left a cruel and unjust legacy as far as the masses were concerned. He clearly wished to have them actively involved in every sphere of Jamaican life. Undoubtedly, he was greatly affected by the efforts of his father whom he admired greatly. The Jamaican masses, as a result of men like Marcus Garvey, Alexander Bustamante and Norman Manley, had achieved a certain level of political

---

117. Economic and Social Survey Jamaica-A government publication-June 1981.

awareness on which Michael Manley might have considered sufficient to build democratic socialism.

However, he later stated:

We paid a high price for our failure to implement and maintain an effective programme of political education during the two years following the announcement of democratic socialism in September 1974.[118]

That price, he thought, resulted in his party's defeat in the elections of 1980 held on October 30,1980. In essence, the people of Jamaica had reached the stage where ideology alone was not enough and the material improvement in their lives seemed impossible to achieve.

Manley summarizes:

We have learned many things. Political ideas and strategy, ideology must be more rigorously defined and taught within the movement. On a general level, political awareness needs to be raised throughout society. Otherwise political movements become the mirrors of popular confusion rather than the mobilisers of change. Economic strategy must be more clearly calculated and the requirements of management more precisely anticipated. Without this, progress cannot be financed and the society at large becomes vulnerable and insecure.[119]

In his book, "Jamaica: Struggle in the Periphery", Michael Manley reflected on his years as Prime Minister of Jamaica from 1972 to 1980. He talked of efforts by external forces to destabilize his government. His seeming lack of control over the security forces and the inability to deal with crime effectively caused many people to feel defenseless in an ever worsening situation. Add to this the fear of a communist style dictatorship, severe food shortages and high unemployment and the future of Jamaica looked gloomy, indeed. The faith and credibility which the people had in

---

118. Michael Manley. Jamaica-Struggle in the Periphery. Great Britain. Oxford Univ. Press. 1982, p. 186

119. Ibid, p.249

Michael Manley from 1972 to 1976 dwindled.

CONCLUSION

Manley's dreams of a just and equitable society where all could live in peace and harmony were not realized through democratic socialism. With the benefit of hindsight and experience, the possibility did exist that he could once again be at the helm of governing Jamaica, especially if the JLP regime was unsuccessful in dealing with the severe economic problems of the country.

In the final analysis, Michael Manley, adamant anti-colonialist, sympathizer of the working man, eloquent and articulate social philosopher, eventually came to realize that economic reform must stand side by side with social reform. Only then will the material well-being of the masses be improved and success as a leader be acknowledged. The Jamaican people have come a long way politically and cherish their democratic right to choose their leader. They value highly the need to have an alternative and the leader must keep this in mind when he advocates an ideology. Only an ideology which results in tangible material gains will be durable.

The main argument of this study has been that Michael Manley and his brand of democratic socialism did not achieve the objectice of improving the material well-being of the masses because of his determined emphasis on the redistribution of existing wealth. In addition, we have observed that (1) Michael Manley and his regime promised more than they could deliver (2)The dismal economic situation which prevailed at the end of the first term of the Manley years made it impossible to institute the social programs that had been envisioned (3) The non-aligned aspect of his foreign policy opened up new areas of communication with non-traditional partners such as Cuba, Hungary, Russia but resulted in lukewarm relations with the United States of America. As a result, the unavailability of funds from international sources had far-reaching implications on national goals (4) Negotiations with the IMF were all-consuming in Manley's second term and were a constant source of controversy (5) Local production fell, local businesses failed, the skilled nationals emigrated taking any available funds with them and leaving the country in serious economic straits (6) The people were active participants in the political arena notwithstanding the high incidence of crime and violence (7) Cultural awareness was advanced through music, art and dance.

The standard of living of the people deteriorated and this was blamed on the leader, Michael Manley, and his democratic socialist ideology. This study has shown that leadership style is crucial if a political ideology is to take hold in Jamaica but that the traditions of the people must also be taken into serious consideration and be incorporated in any new philosophy. Radical change may have to be avoided in fragile economies like Jamaica's. There has been solid advancement on the political and social levels in Jamaica from 1655 on. It will be crucial that future regimes concentrate on advances on the economic level.

EPILOGUE

The People's National Party (PNP), led by Michael Manley, was defeated in the General Elections of 1980 and Edward Seaga, leader of the Jamaica Labour Party (JLP), became Prime Minister of Jamaica. Seaga held that office until December 9, 1989 when the PNP won the General Elections and Michael Manley again became the Prime Minister of Jamaica. The 1983 elections had been boycotted by the PNP.

Manley's philosophy as Prime Minister from 1989-1992 changed from the radical social and economic policies he had postulated between 1972-1980 to a more moderate approach that included encouraging foreign investment. He demonstrated that he had understood where he had gone wrong previously. The world was now a different place, especially after the 1980's, with Ronald Reagan as President of the United States of America and Margaret Thatcher as Prime Minister of Great Britain.

In 1990, Manley instituted a plan to privatize some public services. In 1991, Jamaica was able to reach an agreement with the International Monetary Fund for assistance. Economically, there followed more deregulation and liberalization of funds for Jamaicans and a flat 10% consumption tax replaced eight other taxes and duties.

In 1992, during which political violence in Jamaica escalated, Michael Manley had to relinquish power and his position as Prime Minister of Jamaica because of ill-health. Percival James Patterson of the PNP succeeded Michael Manley as Prime Minister of Jamaica on March 30, 1992.

Michael Manley, born on Wednesday, December 10, 1924, died on Thursday, March 6, 1997, at seventy-two years of age at his home in Kingston, Jamaica. He had served Jamaica as Prime Minister for eleven years.

BIBLIOGRAPHY

Almond, Gabriel A. and Verba. Civic Culture, Princeton, 1963.

Amin, Samir. Unequal Development Monthly Review Press. New York, 1976.

Apter, David. The Politics of Modernization.. University of Chicago Press, Chicago, 1969.

Arawak, Christopher. Jamaica's Michael Manley, Messiah—Muddler—or Marionette. Sir Henry Morgan Press, 1980.

Beckford, G. Persistent Poverty. Oxford University Press. Lond., 1972.

Beckford, George and Witter, Michael. Small Garden—Bitter Weed. Maroon Publishing House, Jamaica, 1980.

Bell, Wendell.Jamaican Leaders. Univ. Of California Press. Calif., 1964.

Boorstern, Edward. Allende's Chile. International Publishers, NY 1977.

Brandel, Fernand.Capitalism and Material Life 1400-1800. Harper & Row, NY., 1973.

Campbell, Angus. et al.,The American Voter. J.Wiley and Sons. NY.1964.

Converse, Philip. " The Nature of Belief Systems in Mass Publics " in D.Apter (ed.) Ideology and Discontent. Free Press. NH., 1964.

Coore, David. Budget Speech. May 16, 1974.

Coore, David. The Jamaica Budget Speech. 1975/1976. May 15th, 1975.

Country profiles-A Publication of the Population Council, Jamaica April. 1971.

Demas, William C. " The Political Economy of the English Speaking Caribbean." Study Paper No.4 Caribbean Ecumenical Consultation for Development.

Eaton, George E. Bustamante and Modern Jamaica. Kingston Publishers Limited. Jamaica 1975.

Economic and Social Survey Jamaica January-June 1981.

Fanon, Frantz. The Wretched of the Earth. Grove Press. NY, 1965.

Fanon, Frantz. A Dying Colonialism. Grove Press. NY, 1965.

Fiedler, Fred E. A Theory of Leadership Effectiveness. McGraw Hill, NY,1967.

Five Year Development Plan 1963-1968, Jamaica

Five Year Development Plan 1978-1982, Jamaica

Garvey, Amy Jacques. Garvey and Garveyism. The Macmillan Co., NY,1963.

Girvan, Norman, and Jefferson, Owen. Readings in the Political Economy
of the Caribbean. New World
Group Ltd. Jamaica 1971.

Hamilton, B.L.St. John. Problems of Administration in an Emergent
Nation.. Praeger. NY, 1964..

Hearne, John ed. The Search for Solutions. Maple House Publishing Co.
Canada, 1976.

Huntingdon, Samuel P. Political Order in Changing Societies.

Hurwitz, Samuel J. and Hurwitz, Edith F. Jamaica .A Historical Portrait.
Praeger, NY, 1971

Irish, M.D. and Prothro, J.W. The Politics of American Democracy
Prentice-Hall, Inc. NJ , 1959.

James, C.L.R. The Black Jacobins. Vintage Books. NY 1963.

Jefferson. O. Post War Economic Development in Jamaica. ISER. 1972.

Kautsky, John H. ed. Political Change in Underdeveloped Countries;
Nationalism and Communism. John Wiley & Sons.
NY, 1963.

Lacey, Terry. Violence and Politics in Jamaica 1960-70. Frank Cass &
Co.

Lewis, W. Arthur. The Theory of Economic Growth. Richard D.Irwin.
Ill., 1955.

Lewis, W. Arthur. Politics in West Africa. Oxford University Press.
NY, 1966.

Leys, Colin.ed. Politics and Change in Developing Countries. Cambridge
University Press, 1960.

Lipset, Seymour. The First New Nation. Basic Books Inc. NY, 1963.

London, Kurt (ed.) New Nations in a Divided World. Praeger, NY, 1963.

Manley, Michael. The Politics of Change. A Jamaican Testament.
Andre` Deutsch, Lond. 1974.

Manley, Michael. A Voice at the Workplace. Andre` Deutsch, Lond.,
1975.

Manley, Michael. Budget Debate Speech. May 29th, 1974.

Manley, Michael. " Democratic Socialism for Jamaica. The Government's
Policy for National Development."

Manley, Michael. " Liberation of the Human Spirit" API, 1977.

Manley, Michael. "Overcoming Insularity in Jamaica." in Foreign Affairs
October, 1980.

Manley, Michael. Jamaica-Struggle in the Periphery. Third World Media,
1982.

Markovitz, Irving L. African Politics and Society: Basic Issues and
    Problems of Government and Development. NY Free
    Press, London. Collier Macmillan, 1970.

Markovitz, Irving L. Power and Class in Africa. Prentice Hall Inc. N.J.
    1977.
Martin, Lawrence. Neutralism and Non-Alignment. Praeger, NY, 1962
Martindale, Colin A. The Role of Sport in Nation Building: A
    Comparative Analysis of Four Newly Developing
    Nations in the Commonwealth Caribbean.
    (Unpublished dissertation) CUNY.1980.
Marx, Karl. The Communist Manifesto. Henry Regnery Co. Ill., 1954.
Mezu, S. O Kechukwu and Ram Desai. Black Leaders of the Centuries.
    Buffalo: Black Academy Press,
    1970.
Munroe, T. The Politics of Constitutional Decolonisation 1944-62.
    Univ. ISER 1972.
Nellis, John R. A Theory of Ideology: The Tanzanian Example. Oxford
    Univ. Press., 1972.
Nettleford, R. (ed.) Manley and the New Jamaica. Longman Caribbean,
    1971.
N Krumah, Kwame. Neo-colonialism: The Last Stage of Imperialism.
    International Publishers, NY, 1965.
Nyere, Julius K. Ujamaa-Essays on Socialism. Oxford Univ. Press, NY,
    1968.
Nyere, Julius K. Freedom and Socialism. Oxford Univ. Press, NY, 1969.
Payer, C. The Debt Trap. Monthly Review Press, NY,1974.
Pye, Lucian.Aspects of Political Development. Little Brown & Co., 1966
Rodney, Walter. How Europe Underdeveloped Africa. London: Bogle-
    L'Ouverture Publications. Dares Salaam: Tanzanian
    Publishing, 1972, Washington D.C. Howard University
    Press, 1974.
Rustow, Dankwart A. ed. Philosophers and Kings. Braiziller. NY 1970.
Sigmund, Paul (ed.) The Ideologies of Developing Nations . Rev.ed.
    Praeger, NY 1967.
Singham, A.W. (ed.) The Non-Aligned Movement in World Politics.
    Lawrence Hill & Co. 1977.
Smith, M.G. The Plural Society in the British West Indies. University
    of California Press, Berkeley, 1965.

Stone, Carl. Class, Race and Political Behaviour in Urban Jamaica.
    Jamaica, ISER 1973.
Stone, Carl and Brown, Aggrey (eds.) Essays on Power and Change in
                    Jamaica. Jamaica Publishing House,
                    1977
The Jamaica (Constitution) Order in Council 1962. Printed by the
    Government Printer, Duke Street, Kingston., Jamaica
Thomas, Hugh. Cuba: Or the Pursuit of Freedom. Eyre and Spottiswoode,
    London, 1971.
Von der Mehden, Fred R. Politics of Developing Nations. Prentice Hall
    Inc. NJ 1964.
Weber, Max. Theory of Social and Economic Organization. NY, 1947.
Wilber. (ed.) The Political Economy of Development and
    Underdevelopment. Random House, NY 1973.
Wilson, Basil. "Surplus Labour and Political Violence in Jamaica. The
    Dialectics of Political Corruption 1966-1976." CUNY
    (unpublished dissertation) 1980.
Williams, Eric. Capitalism and Slavery. University of North Carolina
    Press. NC, 1944.
Wynter, Sylvia. Jamaica's National Heroes Jamaica National Trust
    Commission, 1971.
Zimmerman, L.J. Poor Lands, Rich Lands: The Widening Gap. Random
    House. NY,1965.

PERIODICALS AND NEWSPAPERS

" Jamaica: Address" Vital Speeches 39:75-8. 8/11/72
"Jamaican Joshua." Time 100:23 8/21/72
"Jamaica: a new beginning under new Leadership" Ebony 28:37-40 10/73
"Jamaica: tourist haven with headache galore." U.S. News & World
                    Report.75:63-5. 11/26/73.
"Stalag in Kingston: Gun Court Act" Time 104:55. 9/23/74.
"Reports and Comment: Jamaica. Atlantic 236:22-4. 12/75.
"New Jamaica" Newsweek 87 44-5. 1/12/76.
"Manley Hopes to Use the Soviet Experience" Jamaica Daily News.
                    2/3/77.
"Letter from the Prime Minister."Daily Gleaner. 3/8/77.
"Jamaica Opposition Party Launches 'Peaceful Resistance' to Manley
Rule." Miami Herald 4/20/77.
"PM: Jamaica will continue Struggle," Daily Gleaner. 6/6/77.

"JLP to Boycott Castro's Visit," Ibid. 10/16/77.
"Fidel Comes Today" Ibid.
"Shearer: Socialism Will Not Motivate People to Produce." Ibid. 11/2/77.
"Motion to Censure Seaga Tabled." Ibid.
"Patterson: Seaga Guilty of Misrepresentation." Ibid. 11/7/77.
"Manley, Yugoslav PM Talk Bilateral Co-operation." Ibid. 11/8/77.
"Wide Range to be Explored in Soviet-Jamaica Talks." Ibid. 11/29/77.
"Jamaica Russia Sign Pact." Ibid.
"Cuba, Jamaica Working Out Unified Approach For New Economic Order." Ibid. 2/3/78.
"Middle Classes Caught in Cross-Fire says PM" Ibid.
"Jamaica Aims to Widen Socialist Ties." Ibid. 2/14/78.
"Government Must Reform Itself-NWU" Ibid. 5/18/78.
"IMF Pact Approved by House" Ibid. 5/19/78.
"World Bank to Chair Lending Consortium" Ibid.
"U.S. Economic Mission Comes" Ibid. 7/26/78.
"PM to Visit Moscow April 4-14" Ibid. 3/21/79.
"Government Services Crippled by Strikes" Ibid.
"PSOJ Tells PM About Fear of Links with World Reds" Ibid. 3/24/79.
"PNP Faces a Cross-Roads Decision" Ibid. 3/26/79.
"JLP, Private Sector Denounced by PNP" Ibid. 3/28/79.
"Communism No!" Ibid.
"BITU Knocks 10% Wage Guidelines," Ibid. 4/4/79.
"PM: Would Welcome Co-operation of Opposition." Ibid. 4/7/79.
"New Stone Poll: More Against Than in Favour of PM's Moscow Trip." Ibid. 4/8/79.
"PJ Off to Cuba for talks." Ibid. 4/19/79.
"Prime Minister's Account of Deals with Russia and Hungary." Ibid. 4/20/79.
" Soviet-Jamaica Deal Shocks Trinidad." Ibid. 4/21/79.
"Bid for $25M. From Trinidad Withdrawn." Ibid. 4/21/79.
"Alumina to Russia Won't Affect Deal with Trinidad." Ibid. 4/24/79.
"Patterson States Govts Position in Jamaica-Trinidad Relations." Ibid. 4/28/79.
"Test of Joint Communique on Patterson's Visit to Cuba." Ibid.
"There were no Secret Deals-PJ," Jamaica Daily News. 4/29/79.
Jack Anderson "US Studies Jamaica's Left Turn." reproduced from United Features Syndicate in the Daily Gleaner. 10/30/79.
Ben Meyer. "Pretty Little Jamaica Becomes a Big Worry." Daily Gleaner 11/11/79

"US Pushes Jamaica to Drop Cuba Stand" reproduced from Newsday in Daily Gleaner. 2/20/80.
"The Black Intelligengsia" The Jamaican Weekly Gleaner (NA) 5/26/80.
"Beyond Party Politics." Ibid. 6/2/80.
"Remembering 1938." Ibid.
"Price Controls" Ibid.
"Jamaica's IMF Experience," Ibid.
"Marcus Garvey's Meeting House." Ibid . 7/7/80.
"Our Present Crisis." Ibid.
"Manley and Seaga (Part 2)" Ibid. 8/11/80.
"Elections since Independence." Ibid.
"Making of Modern Jamaica." Ibid. 8/18/80.
"How Seaga Will Rescue the Economy." Ibid.
"Communism and Democracy." Ibid. 9/1/80.
"Victory in Jamaica Exceeds Forecast." NY Times. 11/1/80.

Index

71

MICHAEL MANLEY AND DEMOCRATIC SOCIALISM

Cheryl King's study of Michael Manley's leadership of Jamaica in the 1970's is a well-written and informative study of one of Jamaica's most important post-independence political figures. Ms. King properly starts the study within the historical setting and limitations of Jamaica's colonial experience. The study then moves on to Manley's social democratic thinking and political principles, and his administration's less than successful efforts to work within the powerful and chaotic international environment of the 1970's. Readers will encounter an engaging and wide ranging work of consequence.

William B. Messmer, Ph.D.
Drew University

Cheryl King received her B.A. in Political Science from Hunter College, City University of New York, N.Y., her Diploma in Education (Teaching of English) from The University of the West Indies, Jamaica, West Indies, and her M.A. in Political Science from The Graduate School and University Center, City University of New York, N.Y.
She currently works at the Drew University Library in Madison, New Jersey.